Praise for I Am.

I gave this review of Francis Dale Bennett's book *I Am that I Am: Discovering the love, peace, joy and stability of the True Self* without being solicited to give a review. I think it is a marvelously simple but radical book. Anyone can read this and feel into the direct experience of what he is saying, whether one is a long term spiritual seeker, someone raised in a Christian church, or someone right off the street who has never looked into these things. There is a flow of simplicity and clarity in the pages that made it very readable. I didn't have to stop and ask myself what he meant by certain words. I could see he was using words very lightly, inviting the reader into an always, already present freedom, peeling apart many of the self-beliefs and beliefs about reality that keep so many people spinning their wheels in this lifetime.

Francis' background as a Catholic Monk makes this book even more delicious to me. He has the ability to speak to those in the Christian Church in a way that is fresh and transforming.

Do read this book if you are seeking. It keeps it simple, yet utterly profound.

Scott Kiloby
www.livingrealization.org
www.kiloby.com

I Am
That I Am

Discovering the Love, Peace, Joy and Stability
of the True Self

FRANCIS DALE BENNETT

NON-DUALITY PRESS

This book is dedicated to my brother, Don, who has taught me much about the power of unconditional Love, and to Eric Kolvig, who encouraged me to share what I've experienced.

I AM THAT I AM

First edition published April 2013 by Non-Duality Press

© Francis Bennett 2013
© Non-Duality Press 2013

Cover image: *I Give To You. John 14:27.* VerseVisions Collection. Copyright © 2009 MarkLawrenceGallery.com. All Rights Reserved.

Non-Duality Press | PO Box 2228 | Salisbury | SP2 2GZ
United Kingdom

ISBN: 978-1-908664-29-7

www.non-dualitypress.org

✳ CONTENTS

The whole truth can be summed up in one verse from
the Jewish/Christian scriptures, "I am that I am".
And the entire method for realizing this truth is found
in another of those scriptures,
"Be still and know that I am God."

Sri Ramana Maharshi

GOD IS IN EVERYTHING AND EVERYTHING IS IN GOD

This book is about the greatest, most important discovery ever made. It is about the discovery of the key to happiness and fulfillment. I myself have made this discovery and was overjoyed to do so, but the key to happiness is not a *new* discovery and I am most certainly not the first to have made it, nor will I be the last. Down through the ages many people from every culture, religion and historical setting have made this same, wondrous discovery and, unlike most discoveries in science, mathematics or other fields of knowledge, each one of us has to discover this for ourselves. No one else can do it for you. Hearing about someone else's journey may assist you in making your own, but the only way for you is the path you walk yourself. There is something ironic about discovering this key to happiness: even though we may spend a lifetime looking for it everywhere we can think of, it has always been within us all along. That's precisely why we each must discover this for ourselves.

So let's dispense with all this suspense. About now, you may find yourself asking: *So what is this key to happiness and fulfillment*? Well, the key to happiness and fulfillment is contained in the realization of the following simple truth:

Who you really are, on the most basic level, in your own direct experience, is simple present-moment *awareness*. And the essential true nature of this *awareness* is itself happiness, peace and pure bliss.

So, when I discover who I really am, I immediately discover that I am blissfully happy, because who I am is happiness and bliss. These may seem like pretty big opening claims. But don't take my word for any of this. You can experiment with this on your own and discover for yourself whether or not these claims are true. This little book may be able to assist you in conducting just such an experiment in your own life. That is certainly my hope in writing it.

The 'story of Francis'

I would like to begin by sharing with you a little of the journey that led me to my own discovery. Hopefully, my story will help you along the path to yours. Since I made the discovery that who I really am is present-moment *awareness*, I don't really think too much about my so-called 'personal' history anymore. Recently, I had to put together a résumé so I had to think about where I had been, what I had done, where I went to school, what professional training I had completed. After I finished the résumé and was reading it over to check for possible formatting and spelling errors, it felt like reading a description of somebody else's life or like looking at a kind of simplified, thumbnail sketch of a character in the Cliffs Notes of a novel. So I am about to tell the 'story of Francis'. Of course, none of us are our stories in any absolute sense. Our story is an account of the role we have played on the human stage we call life. However, an interesting character in a story can sometimes point to something beyond the story. All stories we hear in plays, on the screen or in children's books, have something to tell us indirectly. They act as simple pointers. Every story has a moral. We need to look at that to which the story points and not focus too terribly much on the story itself.

I share with you this 'story of Francis' because it may help you, the reader, if I set the scene for the book as a whole. But I share it with the caveat that you do not focus too much on the story itself but simply let it point as it was meant to.

When awakening happens, what we awaken from is an absolute belief in the story. Contrary to popular belief, the story does continue after awakening. The difference is that we then see it for what it is: a simple story. We no longer take it to be reality.

When I was an idealistic young man, a personal quest to experience a greater sense of what I thought of as the *presence of God* led me to the somewhat radical decision to become a Trappist monk at the Abbey of Gethsemani, just a week after my twenty-third birthday.

How did an ordinary, rather sociable, young man come to make this life-changing decision? The seeds were sown when I was a senior in high school. I had been writing religious poetry and songs. My favorite high school English teacher had read some of my poetry and said it reminded him of the work of Thomas Merton, who had been a Trappist monk at a monastery in Kentucky called Gethsemani. The teacher gave me a book by Merton called *The Seven Storey Mountain*. It was an autobiography which told of his spiritual conversion after a life of wild living and partying during his college years in New York City and his subsequent entrance into this Trappist monastery. Merton's life had been pretty different from the somewhat sheltered one I had led up to that point, but he was an intellectual, literary type and I was thinking of myself as a budding intellectual at the time and admired his writing and academic background. I was also fascinated by his descriptions of the monastic life and how the monks lived in silence, dedicating their whole lives to seeking a mystical experience of God's presence. Hearing about all this both fascinated and terrified me at the same time. I was a very social and talkative young man who had many friends and was very involved in a lot of activities, hobbies, music and fun. Even though I was spiritually intense and earnest in my quest to experience the *presence of God* more deeply in my life, the idea of becoming a silent Trappist monk with a shaved head—I had long blond hair that I was very proud of—seemed a little extreme, even for me.

But after high school, while I was attending a college seminary, I began visiting the Abbey of Gethsemani, where Merton had lived and written so many of the books I was now so avidly reading. During many weekends, I would drive down to the monastery in Kentucky from Columbus Ohio. It took me about four hours. I became a regular at the Abbey guesthouse and during the course of several years, I got to know a few of the monks and the vocational director, Brother Giles. They had all known Merton personally and had interesting, humorous stories about him that fascinated me. Merton had become my spiritual hero. By the time I was twenty-two, I had read all of his books and felt an overwhelming attraction to the idea of becoming a Trappist monk myself. After having gotten to know a few of the monks pretty well over several years of visiting the monastery, the prospect of entering the Abbey of Gethsemani was a lot less scary and intimidating. So, in the fall of 1981, I entered the Abbey with the lofty goal of becoming a joyful saint like Saint Francis of Assisi or at least a modern mystic like my hero, Thomas Merton. It was a very idealistic, romantic notion, but I think I was experiencing a genuine earnestness and authentic longing for God that I hoped would be answered by entering the monastery.

Thomas Merton, Zen and the *presence of God*

As I had become more familiar with the whole body of writings that Thomas Merton had produced during his twenty-five or so years as a Trappist monk, I was exposed to his long-standing interest in Eastern spirituality and mysticism. Merton had deeply investigated Zen Buddhism, Hindu Advaita Vedanta and Sufism, the mystical branch of the Islamic tradition. The last portion of writings that Merton produced in the decade before his death were often focused on these various spiritual paths, and his interest in them had left a marked effect on Gethsemani that was still evident in my time there, thirteen years after Thomas Merton's death

When I was a young professed monk at Gethsemani in first, temporary vows, we had a Korean Zen Master coming to the monastery occasionally and giving Zen *sesshins* to any of the monks who were interested in coming. I attended all these little retreats of Soen Sa Nim, the founder of the Providence Zen Center. He had a group of students at the time in nearby Lexington, Kentucky, and so, whenever he came to Kentucky to visit his students there, he would come over to us Trappists and offer us a little retreat and teach us about Zen meditation. I also began corresponding with this Zen Master and tried to see if maybe I could get enlightened like the Zen Buddhist monks I had read about in Merton's book, *Mystics and Zen Masters*.

Several times, when I was practicing Zen and working with this teacher, I had little inspirational glimpses or what the teacher called *satori*, when I suddenly found myself wholly in the present moment. I specifically remember the first one, as I was walking down the stark cloister hallway at Gethsemani just after a Zen retreat with Soen Sa Nim. I wrote the following little poem about this satori.

I am That

Simply, the Sun is beaming in, slanting through the long, clear, narrow windows, as the dust particles dance in the bright, white sunbeams and all there is, in this beautiful, clear light is, THAT.

It was a first, fleeting but wonderful moment of simply being fully, consciously present. These little realizations of *presence* happened many times during my Zen period and I began to make a connection between the experience of present-moment *awareness* and the experience of what I called the *presence of God*—the fleeting glimpses I had had as a young boy and teenager. They seemed to be essentially the same experience, just called by different names. I experienced in both, the same sense of transcendent love and joy and ecstatic awareness, the same sense of *presence*. There was in both experiences a literal *ex-stacy*: a standing out of, or freedom from, the habitual sense of a little 'me'. I had wonderful glimpses that, while experiencing the *presence of God*, or the present-moment *awareness*, there really was no possibility of a petty little person called 'me', with a personal history, a name or role or definable identity. All there was, was *this*. And what *this* was, was the presence of the holy mystery we named God.

After I left the Trappists in 1987 I went back to school, worked, took care of my dad for a time (he had been diagnosed with cancer twice and eventually died of it in 1999). But between 1993 and 1998 I was back with the Trappists several times, this time at a smaller daughter house of Gethsemani in South Carolina.

During those years I became very involved in Vipassana meditation practice and came to meet my friend and teacher, Eric Kolvig. Eric trained at the Insight Meditation Society in Barre, Massachusetts, under the American Vipassana teachers, Joseph Goldstein and Sharon Salzberg. In my day-to-day life in the monastery, I was doing a lot of very simple mindfulness practices, based on the Vipassana techniques. When I had questions or concerns about my practice, I would contact Eric and he would always offer wise advice and assistance. Though I never sat an actual retreat with Eric, he was a mentor and guide for me during those years and I am grateful for the warm spiritual friendship we formed then, and have sustained to this day.

In 1998, I left the Trappist monastery in South Carolina and returned to Columbus, Ohio, to take care of my dad. During that time I met Bhante Henepola Gunaratana, who became my teacher and spiritual friend. 'Bhante G' is a Theravadin Buddhist monk, the oldest living Theravadin elder or *Mahathera*, in North America. He is a very kind, humble, wise and compassionate teacher and was another guide whom I was very fortunate to have met. When my father died in 1999, I went to live for a year with Bhante G at his little forest monastery and retreat center in nearby West Virginia. During that year I received a temporary ordination in his Theravadin monastic lineage and helped him with some of the administrative duties at his center.

During this period of intense Vipassana practice there was a more frequent and sustained *awareness* of being in the present moment and a calmness, clarity and ability to focus developed more fully. And yet, there was still often a sense of suffering and unsatisfactoriness that would arise. Also, the present moment, or 'holy presence', was still playing hide and seek with me most of the time. It seemed that, no matter what I did in the way of practice and no matter how intensely I did it, I was present, then not present, present again and not present again. I frequently had an experience of *presence,* but it was doing a constant appearance and disappearance act. What could I do, what inner work could I undertake, to sustain this experience of *presence*?

Another insight that seemed to arise at this period was the realization that all the stories I continually told myself about everything—stories about myself, God, others, what happened, what didn't happen—were just that: a bunch of stories in my head. I began to see that when I could let the stories go what remained was simply this present moment, right here and now.

All the insights and calmness that had developed over the years were helpful in terms of navigating the inevitable ups and downs of life more smoothly. I had definitely found a certain relative happiness and peace. But I still felt that something indefinable, that I couldn't quite put my finger on, was missing somehow.

In 2000, after the year studying with Bhante G

and the temporary Theravadin ordination, my elderly mother began experiencing a lot of pretty serious health concerns and so I returned to Columbus to take care of her for the next seven years, until her death at age ninety-one. During those years of taking care of my mom, I completed a two year residency in Clinical Pastoral Education (CPE) and worked as a hospital and hospice chaplain. I loved this work and learned so much from the people with whom I was privileged to walk through their experience of terminal illness. I would consider several of them to be real spiritual teachers for me as much as any Zen Master or meditation teacher with whom I had ever worked.

My Zen Master, Mary

Through my years of seeking I worked with several very fine and articulate teachers from whom I learned a great deal of 'spiritual' truth. One of my principal teachers, however, was not a formal spiritual teacher at all. And yet, I would have to say that I learned as much from her as I ever did from any of the classical spiritual masters I was privileged to meet over the years.

I met Mary when I was working as a hospice chaplain. She was originally the patient of another chaplain with whom she had not exactly hit it off. Mary had not felt particularly comfortable with this chaplain, nor was the chaplain particularly comfortable with Mary either! And so the other chaplain had asked me if I would be willing to visit her, just to see if the two of us might be able to establish a better rapport. However, she made this request coupled with a warning. She told me that Mary was a forty-three year old wife and mother, with an invasive and fast-growing form of cancer of the tongue that was now spreading into her face. The chaplain said, "This patient is a very bitter woman who is angry at God for permitting this disease in her life, and she is looking for answers that no one can really give her, and she seems to be projecting her anger at God onto whoever she sees as God's representative (aka, the chaplain). Sooo, good luck!"

It had started with a lesion on the tongue that Mary's dentist had noticed and had some concerns about. They got a biopsy done and, just as the dentist had feared, it was cancer—a very rare and virulent kind. By the time I came to see Mary, half her face was already gone and she was in the final weeks of her life. When I entered the living room of Mary's home, where her husband had set up a hospital bed for her, I saw a petite woman in a beautiful chiffon negligee with a gauzy, flower print veil covering up the lower half of her face beneath her eyes. Peering at me from over the veil was a set of the most beautiful green/blue eyes I had ever seen, with long dark eyelashes and carefully arched eyebrows. There was a picture on the wall of a lovely young woman from what seemed like a different lifetime, with the same beautiful eyes, smiling and surrounded by her young family in front of the Enchanted Castle at Disney World. As I walked into the room, Mary held up a carefully crafted sign that said *Hello!* Since she no longer had a tongue or lower jaw, she could only communicate by writing on a tablet or holding up little signs she kept within reaching distance beside her bed. I told her I was the hospice chaplain, introduced myself and told her we could visit a little if she wanted to. Once she knew I was the chaplain, she wasted no time in any social niceties. She picked up her writing tablet and wrote a heart-wrenching question: *Why is God allowing this to happen to me?* I immediately felt a wave of sorrow and compassion wash through my whole being. "I don't know," I said after a few seconds of eye contact. I continued, "Mary, I really don't know, but if you want to explore this question more deeply together, we can." After a few more questions between us, we ended our first meeting.

Most of the time, I could visit patients during the day and be very present with them during these visits. Even though I would be fully engaged with the person in the moment, when I went home at night, I was generally quite able to let go of my thoughts about them and focus on being present with my elderly mother, for whom I was primary caregiver. With Mary, things were different somehow. Even after that first meeting, I seemed to think about her and her question many times a day. Even for me, that question was a bit like one of those formal Zen koans I had worked on with my Zen teachers. The koan is an enigmatic question that, on a logical/rational level, really has no answer at all. One sits with the koan until there is a breakthrough with it. One answers the question by transcending it as a question. The answer to a koan is that there is no answer in any sense that is satisfying to the rational mind. My Zen teacher used to say, "You must *become* the question." Life had given Mary a very mysterious and challenging koan and she had certainly become this question. She lived and breathed her koan every moment of every day. She was wrestling with her koan as intensely and passionately as any serious Zen student could ever hope to.

Mary and I began to form a kind of liturgy, a ritual, in our visits. It went like this; I would enter the room. Mary would hold up her *Hello!* sign. I would smile. She would generally write on her tablet: *How's your mother?*

I would give her the latest report on mom's health and ask her how her family was doing. She would give me the latest reports on them and after a brief pause, she would begin to write her koan. It was usually not the same direct question of *Why?* which she had penned on the first day. Normally it took the form of a bitter complaint against God. I was just fine with that. I could understand why she was bitter. It all seemed very unfair to her and to those around her. She was a lovely, good and decent person who had done her best to be a good wife and mother, a good neighbor and a good Christian. This thing called cancer seemed to her like a malicious thief that had snuck in through the back door of her life and was hell-bent on taking from her everything she dearly loved.

In the formation I had experienced in my CPE residency, we were reminded again and again that giving pat and standard answers to life's more thorny questions was seldom really helpful. It was emphasized that most people who are suffering seem to find some therapeutic comfort in the simple reality of being listened to and truly heard. They have a very personal story of suffering and misery that often has no possibility of a material or physical resolution. People suffering from a terminal illness, as the very name suggests, are all too aware that they are inexorably headed toward a terminus, an inevitable end-game. So, they either give up in a kind of despair, or they slowly learn to draw on all the spiritual, psychological and material resources they may have at their disposal. Mary had the resources of a fine intellect and the strong character traits of curiosity, a sense of justice and love for her family. All these characteristics came into play in her desperate attempt to make sense of what was happening to her and her family in terms of this disease that seemed to be invading her life.

One day I went to visit Mary as usual. That morning I had attended mass and found myself gazing up at the large, life-size Spanish crucifix that adorned the wall of the church I normally attended. The Christ on the cross was bloody and beat-up. It was not one of these sanctimonious, sanitized versions of Christ on the cross, with a serene look gazing placidly out on the world. The Christ on this cross was clearly in great pain. His face was not serene, but rather contorted in a grimace. His body was pitifully bruised and broken. Looking at this man on the cross, I thought of my friend Mary. I could almost hear the words of Jesus from the cross, spoken so many centuries before, "My God, my God, why have you forsaken me?" In that moment I had the thought that Mary had indeed received the very same koan from the Father that Jesus himself had received. And I had been given this koan from Mary in a lineage of pain and suffering. In that moment, I knew she was an important teacher for me.

When I got to Mary's house later that morning, we began our usual liturgy without delay. She was writing out her usual lament against God, like a passage from the book of Job. I was sitting there listening, or rather reading, May's written comments, as I usually did. Suddenly words were coming out of my mouth that I had absolutely not planned on saying at all. Normally I would allow her lament against God to simply play itself out. It seemed to generally go on for about twenty to thirty minutes. Her husband would then come in and give her some medication or other, we would all visit together for a few more minutes and I would leave. But on this day there was a different energy in the air.

From the time I entered her room that morning, it was as if the image of Jesus on the cross was superimposed upon the person of Mary herself. Whenever I looked at her I saw the same image of the suffering Christ I had seen that morning. The atmosphere in the room seemed charged with a sacred presence that day. About ten minutes into her lament I heard strange words suddenly coming out of my mouth.

I said to her, "Mary, I can hear how painful and difficult your experience is right now. Do you want to be free from all this pain?" She set down the writing tablet and stared at me, her eyes brimming with tears as she shook her head up and down indicating a *yes* in response to my question. Her eyes were filled also with something else besides tears, something new I had never seen before. There was a tenderness in her expression and perhaps a kind of expectancy of some kind. I had never asked her a question like this before. Normally I just listened. I think she was curious about what I was going to say next, but not any more curious than I was myself! My experience after that was that time seemed to proceed in slow motion. Words were coming out of my mouth, but there were no thoughts forming in my head beforehand. The words were simply appearing in the room and I was listening to them arrive as if someone else were speaking them. I realized that I also had tears in my eyes as I spoke these words and there was an overwhelming feeling of love that was saturating the room. I heard the following words being said and the words themselves were arising out of this presence of all-pervading love.

I said, "Mary, the only way I know of to get beyond the kind of pain you are experiencing right now, is the way of absolute surrender."

Just as soon as I spoke these words, I began to wonder if I had made a grave mistake. By that time Mary and I had established a kind of trust, and yet I wondered if she might be offended by these words and ask me to leave her house. Wasn't I giving her one of those pat, standard answers that my CPE supervisors had warned me about? I didn't really know for sure. But one thing I *did* know. The words had already been spoken. They were still lingering in the room like the tell-tale tone of the little high-pitched gong my old Zen master would strike at the beginning and end of a meditation session. I couldn't take these words back. All I could do was to wait for Mary's response. Her beautiful eyes filled up more fully with tears and the tears began brimming over and rolled down her cheeks into the sheer silk flowers of her face veil. We just gazed at each other for probably three minutes or so and, at the end of three minutes, she wrote something on her writing tablet and held it up for me to see. It said: *Thank you Francis!*

Mary had surrendered completely and utterly that day. She seemed to be a different person. All the bitterness disappeared and an unconditional joy appeared in its place. Her birthday was about two days after this event and it was the most joyous party I had ever attended. There was a presence of peace and joy that surrounded Mary from that day forward that was palpable. Everyone around her could feel it. When I visited her after that day, I felt absolutely uplifted in her presence. She was transfigured, radiating a living light and peace and serenity. The next week she wrote on her tablet: *I used to ask God and myself every day, Why me? Now I find myself saying, Why **not** me?* This statement, coming from a woman who, just a week before, was so bitter and angry at God, seemed truly incredible to me, like a miracle. She had definitely 'passed' the koan that the cancer had given her.

Mary only lived about two more weeks after this breakthrough.

Are you going to wait until you are about to die to surrender, or will you do it now?

Soon after her death I was driving in my car and suddenly felt an overwhelming sense of the same *presence* that seemed to surround her in her final weeks. I was so overcome with emotion that I had to pull the car over and get ahold of myself in order to continue driving. The following strange question formed itself in my mind: *Are you going to wait until you are about to die to surrender, or will you do it now?* I didn't answer the question with words, but there was a kind of emotional and spiritual release that happened there on the side of the road that seemed to be a kind of watershed moment for me. The fruit of this experience was that, from that day to this, I have had a deep sense that what I used to think of as 'my life' was really no longer mine and that all was unfolding somehow as it was meant to, simply as it had to. How did I know this? Because whatever was unfolding was, and is, simply the way it is right now. How could it possibly be otherwise? There hasn"t been very much worry since then, even when things are not going as I might prefer. There is an overwhelming sense that what I used to think of as my life really has very little to do with 'me'. Life lives itself seemingly through this 'me', but none of it is any of my business! This is not to say that I no longer do what I can to try to improve some situation or other, or to act for the best in all circumstances. Paradoxically, this seeming intention toward change is still a normal response to certain situations. But there is a kind of ground of deep acceptance and profound surrender that permeates life and makes even the challenging times much more livable. I attribute all of this, with deep gratefulness and palms held high together, to my Zen Master, Mary, of the beautiful green/blue eyes. I will never forget her.

I learn about self-investigation

After my mom died in 2007, I entered Roman Catholic monastic life again. This time at a little monastic community that was originally founded in France. They had made a small foundation in Montreal in 2004, which is where I entered. Here I discovered the teaching of Bhagavan Sri Ramana Maharshi. He had lived and died in India some years before I was even born, but I would certainly consider him one of my most important teachers, perhaps even the most significant teacher I ever had. Even though he was a Hindu, Sri Ramana taught me the most about what, I have come to believe, was Jesus' essential message and the good news about who we all really are in our deepest heart. I had heard of Sri Ramana before, when I was a Trappist at Gethsemani, and had seen photos of his face, with its extraordinary luminous serenity, but I had never gone deeply into his teachings. Now I ran across a little book called *The Spiritual Teaching of Ramana Maharshi* and I found that his simple method of 'self-inquiry' struck a chord for me. This is a very simple spiritual practice that I actually prefer to call self-investigation or self-abiding because I believe these words more accurately describe what happens in this practice. A more complete description of the practice can be found elsewhere in this book, but there are hints of it in virtually anything I have to say about spiritual practice.

God is in everything and everything is in God

I was happily living the monastic life again and trying to practice the self-abiding I had learned from Sri Ramana. It was a serene and happy time. Several years into all this, I experienced what I could only call a deep awakening that changed my whole world. This was a major shift in perception that was incomparable to anything I had ever previously experienced in all my years of seeking and practice. In fact, this so-called experience was not an experience at all, but was rather the simple discovery of the pure *awareness* in which every experience rises and sets.

At one point, right in the midst of Mass, it was as if a bolt of lightning had struck the crown of my head and sent a strong energy current through my whole body, from head to feet. I suddenly clearly saw, in that instant, that in reality, the *presence of God* that I had been seeking my whole life had actually always been already within me and all around me: *God is in everything and everything is in God.*

Why hadn't I been able to see this before? It was so obvious. And this was not merely some kind of philosophical or theological concept. I clearly *saw* this and felt it with every fiber of my being.

There was a deep intuitive knowing in that instant that my own most basic sense of simple existence or beingness, the *I am* or the Self that Sri Ramana had taught so much about, is, in fact, always, effortlessly, eternally present here and now. There is simply no possibility of it ever not being present. And this simple sense of *presence* in the eternal now is nothing other than the *presence of God.* Simultaneously included in this split second seeing and knowing was the under-standing that this eternally shining presence of *I am* was and is and always will be my own true identity.

The 'story of me' fell away utterly and completely. I could still remember facts of personal history, but there was no longer any personal identification with any of it. I saw clearly in that instant that any 'story of me' was simply a concept in the head, having absolutely no foundation in living reality. All of this happened in a fleeting, lightning flash in time, and beyond time, and yet it was indelibly marked on my deepest conscious-ness. It has never left me since. In that instant, I saw that who I am is simply this eternally existing, simple presence of *awareness.* I am the *I Am*; nothing more, nothing less. It seems that, once clearly seen in this way, it is not really possible ever to un-see this Truth.

This realization is, by its very nature, the realiza-tion of true love, peace, joy, and vast spaciousness. For lack of a better term, I sometimes call it the realization of our true nature as God's beloved child. But all of these words and metaphors can only poorly point to this reality, this *silence,* which is entirely beyond words.

I hope that this brief account of my so-called 'life', together with what I have shared in the pages that follow, will help point you toward the true Self that dwells deep in the heart of each one of us. The writing of this little book is a feeble attempt to share with you what I have come to know of this true Self or *pres-ence* that we all already are, as God's beloved child. I have found that the true Self is, in fact, the wondrous discovery of all the love, peace and joy that you and I have been so earnestly seeking our whole life long. The truly ironic thing is that it has never left us for one moment of our existence. It never could and never will leave us because, in the most profound sense, it is us. It is life or existence itself, which is really what and who we all are.

The fruits of awakening

Awakening is a waking up to the reality of the absolute, and yet there are certain results of awakening on the relative level of life. It's quite natural for us to want to be happy, free from care and anxiety. We search and search to find these blessings and we continually think we will find them in some person, place or thing. But when we awaken to the absolute level of reality and see it with great clarity, we are not only seeing clearly the absolute, we are also seeing clearly the relative. There is really no problem with the relative. The only 'problem' we have with the relative is when we wish for the relative to be absolute. Once we see with clarity the relative nature of all the forms appearing and disappearing in this physical world we live in, we no longer feel the need to insist that they be in any way different than what they are. We now learn to accept the temporary, ephemeral nature of the relative world and we see no problem with it.

It's just like when we receive a rose from someone on a special occasion. We love receiving the rose and we enjoy its beauty. But we never expect that rose to be around twenty years from now, do we? No, we know full well that the rose is temporary and fleeting. Its evanescent nature is actually part of its beauty.

So an awakening to the absolute level of reality is also an awakening to the relative level. All anxiety is basically caused by our wanting reality to be other than it is. What we come to see is that the relative is not separate from the absolute at all. The relative is simply a temporary manifestation happening within the space of absolute consciousness/awareness. All the relative forms that exist in our experience must arise and cease in the absolute spaciousness of awareness. So all forms, all physical manifestations are actually, and paradoxically, part of the formless.

Awakening brings with it the realization that while, relatively speaking, many things matter in life and have a certain heavy portentousness or emotional urgency, they do not matter in the same way, absolutely speaking. This helps us hold all the forms that arise in our experience in a much lighter manner. Things, people and events that used to bother us don't seem to have nearly the impact on us that they once did. There is so much less anxiety and life is consequently navigated more easily.

Most of us are looking for stability and peace. Once we realize the absolute level of reality, we are plugged in to the source and summit of stability and peace. Spacious awareness is the one stable, unchanging reality. When our focus is rooted in simple awareness rather than in all the appearances arising and ceasing in that awareness, we realize that stability is always present. We realize that we ourselves are stability itself.

When we learn to live in the spacious stillness and silence of the absolute, we begin to learn how to listen, because we come to realize that the silence that we are on the absolute level is always listening. This is a great help in the cultivation of healthy human relationships. Many people go through life feeling unheard. Many people don't really listen to others too well. They are so busy composing some kind of response to what they think the other person is saying that they don't have much energy left to actually listen to another.

The other way in which awakening assists us in the area of relationships is that we realize that no person on the planet is ever capable of really satisfying us or making us happy in any ultimate sense. This takes an awful lot of pressure off of a relationship. If we are not looking to the other person to fulfill us, we can begin to relax and enjoy them just as they are.

When you know with deep certitude that your essential being of spacious awareness is actually not separate from the reality of God, the source of ultimate happiness and peace, you come to realize, in your direct experience, the absolute happiness and peace for which you have been searching the world over.

Right now, with absolutely no effort on your part, a peaceful joy and happiness is already present at the very core of your being. This peaceful joy and happiness is the essence of who you are on the very deepest, most absolute level of your being. This joy and happiness is entirely unconditional. That is to say, it has absolutely no dependency on conditions at all. The ultimate fruit of awakening is this abiding, unconditional joy and happiness. This joy and happiness is actually your undeniable heritage as God's beloved child. You are, in fact, yourself infinite love, joy and happiness. Realizing this truth is perhaps the most wonderful, practical result of awakening. After all, isn't every human being on the face of the planet seeking happiness and peace? Some would even say that this pursuit of happiness is the whole reason any of us are here in the first place.

My deepest intention is to dedicate what remains of this life to sharing with you the liberating truth of who you really are. All you are seeking is already fully within you. My deepest wish for you is that, as you read this little book, you may wake up and realize who and what you are already, who you always have been.

CHAPTER 1

SHIFT: PAYING ATTENTION TO WHAT IS ALREADY HERE

Sometimes we overlook the most obvious things. It really all depends on where we place our attention. It's like being in a movie theatre watching a movie you are intensely interested in. Once the movie has started, you don't really notice the movie screen at all. And yet none of the scenes in the movie could appear before you without the screen. The screen is the backdrop of the entire movie. Of course the movie is your primary focus, so you tend to look right past the screen. But the screen is what makes the experience of the movie possible.

During the entire course of the movie, the screen is present, yet, at the same time, it is entirely unaffected by what appears on it. An idyllic, romantic scene can appear on the screen or a nightmarish, tragic scene can appear on the screen, but the screen always remains the same, no matter what happens to be appearing on it.

Our simple presence/awareness/consciousness, that which knows all that arises in experience, is likewise always here and now. This *awareness* is the backdrop of every experience as it comes and goes within it. The simple fact that *awareness* is always present, underneath every experience, shows us that there is a stable, unchanging, true essence. This has been called the true Self, or our 'spirit'. I like to call it 'God's beloved child'. All of us are already that, whether we are aware of it consciously or not. Nothing can ever change this reality of who we really are. Whether you feel aware or unaware, this simple consciousness of pure *awareness* is actually always aware—aware even of your apparent non-awareness. This *awareness* can never fail to be present. It could even be called your most basic, essential sense of existence. Can you ever manage to exist more than you already exist? Or is it possible to exist less? So it is equally quite impossible for the simple presence of *awareness* to ever be more present or less present. *Awareness* is, in fact, the foundation, the bedrock, on which every single experience rests. Experiences come and experiences go, thoughts come and thoughts go, emotions come and emotions go, but the one remaining reality behind them all is the simple, clear, ever present, ever peaceful *awareness* which knows all of them. Any spiritual practice worth its salt simply teaches you to shift your attention to this underlying pure *awareness*, just as in the midst of a movie you might suddenly shift your attention toward the screen on which you are watching the movie.

I had a very graphic experience of this analogy in the 1980s. I was with some college friends at a showing of *The Rocky Horror Picture Show*, a cult classic film, made in the 1970s. Some of the audience used to dress up like characters in the film and would physically interact with the story appearing on the screen. It was a lot of fun to see such a strange spectacle unfold in an ordinary movie theatre in Columbus, Ohio. Sometimes the more dedicated members of the audience would get a little carried away, spraying the other audience members with water, for example, during the rain storm scene. Most people, if they were smart, took umbrellas to the showings of this film, or at least wore no expensive clothes. One night while I was at the film (we would all sometimes go on Saturday nights when we had nothing better to do), I witnessed a member of the audience take a bucket of some kind of red liquid and suddenly pitch it all over the bottom of the screen. Needless to say, we all suddenly shifted our attention from the movie we were watching *on* the screen to the presence of the screen itself. The young guy who did this was unknowingly playing the role of a spiritual teacher or a spiritual practice. He was quite force-fully shifting our attention from one level of reality to another. If my memory serves me correctly, he was dressed as a vampire.

No matter what you are experiencing, try to begin to shift your attention from exclusively focusing on the experience to that which is aware of the experience as well. Simply notice that which is knowing an experience in any given moment. Notice right now, for example, that which is looking at the words on this page. Your thoughts and experiences are constantly changing, always arising and passing away, but that which knows them all is ever the same. It never arises and passes away because it is always present. This noticing of the *awareness* that is already always present is actually the essence of all spiritual practices. And perhaps, paradoxically, this simple noticing is also the goal of all spiritual practices. The path and the goal sometimes seem quite distinct, but in this case, they are not two, but one. In the authentic spiritual life the journey and the destination are always really one and the same.

This natural *awareness* that is always present at the core of any and every experience you could possibly ever have is open, unconditioned and pure. It is like the empty space in a room. When you are looking around a room, you would normally not notice the space in the room, unless you are a feng shui expert. Most people are much more interested in the objects appearing in the room. Most people see rooms every day and completely ignore the space in those rooms. Just take a minute and look around the room you are in right now, or even around the park or outdoor scene that may be appearing before you. Instead of focusing exclusively on all the objects you see appearing in the space, notice the space itself all around the objects. Simply shift your perspective a little. When you really consider it, space (which seems empty, although science tells us it is not really so) is everywhere we look. And isn't the space in our universe absolutely necessary in order for any object to exist? Just as the space in a room is completely unaffected by what happens in the room, so the clarity and purity of *awareness* is wholly unaffected by whatever arises in it. No experience leaves any trace on the clear, pure *awareness* in which it arises. Even in the midst of the most seemingly difficult experience, we may begin to shift our attention and notice more and more the simple presence of that which knows the experience, instead of just the experience.

Of course, this does not mean that we now need to ignore experiences. Our attention to the experience is still there and the experience may even be calling for a response, but the focus on the experience is somehow softer. We begin to notice and rest more fully in the peaceful *awareness* in which every experience comes and goes.

We begin to focus on the unchanging *presence* that knows every experience. We have inadvertently discovered the *presence of God*. When we make this amazing discovery we simultaneously learn that we can be happy, no matter what. This sense of 'just being' is always right in the middle of what we call 'well-being' because, no matter what is happening, life is always still living, existence is still existing, *presence* is constantly present. As the old saying goes, "God's in his heaven (which is always actually here and now) and all's right with the world." Or as the wonderful mystic Julian of Norwich put it, "All shall be well, and all shall be well, and all manner of thing shall be well."

The open spacious presence of *awareness* can contain any experience whatsoever. This open spacious presence is actually who you are on the deepest level. It is the true Self within us all. It is the *Imago Dei*, the image and likeness of God within us. It is God immanent. In Hinduism it is called *atman*, which means our indwelling divinity. Once we see this clearly, we are free. We see that the presence of *awareness* can accommodate absolutely anything that arises in our experience and we are at peace. We may still sometimes not feel very peaceful emotions, but the spaciousness of our *awareness* can contain even that experience of non-peace.

This *awareness* is itself the peace of God that passes all understanding.

This open *awareness* in which all things arise and cease, in which all appears and disappears, cannot really be defined as any object. It transcends the concepts of subject and object. This reality can be known in a certain sense, but not at all objectively. We 'know' *awareness* by simply *being awareness* and, lucky for us, we already are that. So there's really no need to become somebody different.

Some people, down through the ages, have named this ever present, unchanging *awareness*, or pure consciousness, 'God', but it's important that we remember that the word 'God' is only a word and, as a word, it can never contain or define the holy mystery to which it points. Throughout all of history people have been seeking God everywhere—sometimes frantically, fanatically and single mindedly. The irony is that the simple *awareness* which is conscious of our seeking is itself the very reality we seek. We are a lot like the little fish in the great ocean that was swimming constantly back and forth, here and there, desperately looking for something. One of the other fish, noticing his friend's frantic search, grew concerned and asked him what it was he was seeking. The little fish answered, "I am looking for the Great Ocean. I simply must find it. I can't possibly live without it. I'll never be happy until I find the Great Ocean. This alone is my life's goal."

So, if we are seeking this *awareness* or the *presence of God* and it is, in fact, already always here and now, how do we go about recognizing it? Just consider what advice you might offer the little fish. You'd probably say something like: *Hey friend, relax! Stop this frantic seeking and just rest in the reality that already surrounds you. The Great Ocean is all around you and within you. You yourself are a part of the Great Ocean. You couldn't get away from the Great Ocean if you tried.*

So maybe you yourself can take the advice you might have offered to the stressed-out little fish. Start trying to simply relax into the *awareness*, the knowing, that is already, always present. It's really quite simple and accessible. You are already the presence of *awareness*; effortless, unchanging, rock-solid and stable. Your *awareness* is like a great mountain. You yourself are this mountain of *awareness*. Allow yourself to rest in this fact and this peaceful *presence* will permeate and overtake your entire life. You will live in a peace and joy that has nothing to do with your thoughts or experiences. All kinds of thoughts and experiences and feelings will still certainly come and go. But in the midst of them all, you will discover the peace and joy and bliss of the true Self that has always been there all along. This peaceful space of *awareness* never goes away because all that comes and goes has to arise within it. No matter what comes your way, no matter how upsetting it seems, you can know: *I am the open, peaceful* awareness *in which this thing appears and disappears.*

When you really know this, you will experience a stability in your life that you may have never dreamed possible. More and more you will learn to rest in this *awareness* and even to trust it. You will not have to search for some special, esoteric 'spiritual state'. You will learn to practice this *presence* in every state, in the midst of all experiences, good or bad, happy or unhappy, 'spiritual' or 'mundane'. You will come to see that practicing this *presence* is truly the practice of the *presence of God.*

I want to share with you a mathematical formula that I have discovered that has transformed my life. Though I must admit, I am not the first to discover this formula. The formula is this:

Pure, Clear Awareness = The Presence of God.

And remember, pure, clear *awareness* is always with you so consequently God is always with you. But the choice is always yours. You can learn to recognize this ever present *presence of God* which seems always to remain beyond, yet is always within. Paradoxically, it is both transcendent and immanent at the same time. It is greater than what you think 'you' are, yet, on the deepest level, it is not at all separate from you either. Usually, sometime after we begin to recognize that *awareness* in which all appears and disappears, we also begin to notice that all this seemimgly diverse stuff that is appearing in the space of *awareness* is not really separate from the space in which it appears. Another big shift in perception. In other words, there really is no separation between subject and object. Some spiritual paths, and even some psychological therapies, teach people to develop the perspective of the silent witness or 'watcher.' It is a practice that can be very helpful for those who find themselves feeling somewhat overwhelmed by what happens to be arising in their experience. But if we stop at this, witness-consciousness stage, we can begin to cultivate a very detached and unengaged, dualistic attitude toward life. From this dualistic perspective, life is divided up into two categories:

Category #1: Me (the observer or subject)
Category #2: Everything else in the universe

But as we live more and more from the perspective of the silent observer, we begin to see that there really is no observer apart or separate from what is observed. There is no subject apart from an object, no seer apart from the seen. Another way to say this is that there is no observer or observed at all, but there is just 'observing'. The knower and the known become one in the knowing—although there has never been a 'becoming' because it has always been so.

In India, those who wake up to this truth are called *jnanis*, which could be translated as knowers or the ones who know. Some people think that these *jnanis* are very special, rare and holy beings who become knowers of reality only after a long, arduous spiritual journey that usually involves spending a great deal of time as a hermit in a cave and many years living under a vow of silence ... in fact, we are all already knowers, we just don't know it yet.

Jesus said, "Unless you become like a little child, you can never enter the kingdom of heaven." Did you ever notice that little children and babies have not yet developed any concepts like subject and object, me and you, tree or house? Consequently they don't see life as a problem to be solved or conquered. Sure they get hungry or wet in their pants and feel uncomfortable, but when they do, they simply cry. It's no problem, at least not for them. They feel no particular need to categorize, define or set agendas for life. So, they are generally quite content and happy just *being*. Look into the innocent, open face of a baby sometime and you will see the serene and mysterious smile of a little Buddha. That's why so many of us are attracted to little babies. They seem to never be separate from life. They simply *are* life. Of course they also smell so good—at least, most of the time.

Perhaps Jesus' idea of becoming like a little child was pointing to this reality of innocent, pure *presence*. This *presence* is still in every one of us, it simply seems to have become covered over. We learn language and concepts and complicated stories about life as we grow up and this distracts us from our natural sense of pure *presence*. We start to overlook this simple wonder of *presence* that always remains underneath all the stories.

But if you begin to stop separating yourself from life, if you become like a simple little child, simply present in this moment, then life will begin to reveal itself to you and the wonder and joy that has never left you will be dis-covered again.

There simply is no separation anywhere to be found. Life, all of life, is simply that all-inclusive *awareness* in which everything is appearing and disappearing. Your true Self is this *awareness*. It is the love, joy, peace and wonder that you see in the eyes of little babies and saints. It is all you have been searching and longing for, whether your particular search has been 'mundane' or deeply 'spiritual'. This *awareness* has never left you for one moment of your existence. This is the ironic truth about life that often seems to arrive only at the end of a grueling search. Was the search necessary? Yes and no. In reality this *awareness*, this love and peace and joy, were always effortlessly present all along. But maybe you had to look everywhere else for it before you realized that it's always been within you. Who knows? This is always the million dollar question: *Who is it that knows?* And, if you answer this question, you will have solved the Rubik's Cube we sometimes call 'life'.

Just try to remember the advice you would give the little fish:

Hey, relax my friend! Learn to rest in the fact that the holy mystery is all around you and within you. You yourself are part of the holy mystery. You couldn't get away from it if you tried. Be at peace in wellbeing, because your being is always well. You are already always where you want to be, whether you realize it or not. Just enjoy it. Learn to just be happy, because unconditional happiness is your true nature. You are already, all the love, joy, peace and stability you seek. You are and have always been and always will be, the beloved child of God, infinitely loved by God. You are the child of pure awareness. *You are love itself.*

✳ CHAPTER 2

THE SEARCH FOR HAPPINESS

Every living being longs always for a happiness untainted by sorrow; and everyone has the greatest love for himself, which is solely due to the fact that happiness is his real nature.

Bhagavan Sri Ramana Maharshi

What is the one common motivating force behind all human endeavor and all the many and varied human behaviors and pursuits we observe going on around us each day? Isn't it the simple goal of feeling happiness? Whatever we do as human beings, whether we call it 'virtuous' or 'sinful', good or bad, unselfish or selfish, everything from robbing a bank to feeding the homeless, we do it all because on some level we believe the action will bring happiness. And whose happiness is by far the most important to us as individuals? If I as an individual am really honest, I must admit that it is my own happiness that matters most to me. Some people will deny this but, if we look at it closely, it seems pretty obvious and undeniable.

However altruistic and unselfish we may believe our primary motivation in life to be, even our generous acts of kindness are clearly deeply motivated by this personal desire for happiness as well. Don't you generally feel good when you do something unselfish and nice for somebody else? Therefore there is always at least some aspect of seeking your own happiness in all of your unselfish, altruistic actions. Even the example of a self-sacrificing parent, fully dedicated to the welfare of their child, can illustrate this point. This self-sacrificing parent may give quite generously and lovingly of their energy, time, money, all for the welfare of their beloved child. They may even be willing to die for their child if necessary. As noble and altruistic as these kinds of actions may be, if we analyze them deeply and honestly, we must acknowledge that, while there is certainly a genuine concern for the child in question, the self-sacrificing parent also does all these things because doing so brings them a certain feeling of happiness and peace. If they failed to do these things, they would most likely feel that they were not a good parent and would feel unhappy and guilty.

The parent in this example feels unhappy when they see their beloved child unhappy or in some kind of need. So their own sense of unhappiness over their child's unhappiness is also motivating them to alleviate the child's suffering, even at the cost of inconvenience or suffering for themselves. They may, in fact, even experience a genuinely positive sense of emotional pleasure or comfort in their personal suffering if they really believe that it is contributing to the alleviation of their child's actual or potential suffering.

And why is it that even our wishes for other people's happiness are, in reality, ultimately connected to our personal desire for our own? Quite simply, it is because we naturally and instinctively cherish and love ourselves more than we love or cherish any other person. Jesus' injunction to love your neighbor as yourself pre-supposes the universal primacy of this self-cherishing attitude. If you doubt that this is true, honestly observe any human being, including yourself, for one full day and take notes. See what you think then.

The truth is that we ultimately love the other people, places or things we love because we believe they will make us happy. This motivation can sometimes be quite subtle and not immediately obvious to others or even to ourselves, yet it is there nonetheless. We can readily admit that the love we feel for possessions, certain places or situations, pastimes and hobbies, favorite foods or musical groups is because we believe they may be a potential source of personal happiness or pleasure. No one would seriously dispute this. Why else would we spend our time and energy doing these things or pursuing these personal activities or interests? But if we look honestly at the question, we may begin to see that this is also true of the love we feel for the people in our personal lives as well. We somehow feel that this is narcissistic or selfish. Even though this self-interest is quite normal and central to all of us, many of us develop unrealistic ideals of spiritual altruism that deny this reality. For example, we can't imagine saying to someone we love: *If I had to choose between you and my ultimate happiness, I would most definitely choose my own happiness over you.*

And yet, this is a perfectly normal and even healthy mindset.

Most of us would, of course, never make such a statement to someone we love and would, in fact, think such a statement to be the height of egoism and selfishness. Imagine how we would feel if someone we love said to us: *I want you to choose **me** over and above your own personal happiness. I am more important than* *whether or not you **ever** experience happiness in life and I want you to know that and always keep that in mind when you are dealing with me.*

Wouldn't we somehow honestly feel that such a person was being very unreasonable and demanding?

So our love for our own happiness seems to be inseparable from our love for any person, place or thing. All our likes and dislikes, our fears and desires seem to be rooted in our love and concern for our own happiness. Hopefully we are beginning to see here that all that we love, be they people, places or things, we love precisely because we believe they may be sources of happiness for us.

So why do we seem to be made this way? Why is it that we all seem to instinctively love ourselves more than anything or anyone else? As I have already stated several times now, the reason we love anything at all is because we believe the thing we love may bring us happiness. So, could this principle hold true for the love we have for ourselves as well?

Since we all love ourselves first, before anything else, we seem to have a deep intuitive sense that we ourselves are the greatest source of true happiness among all the other potential sources of happiness. This primary self-cherishing attitude seems to be truly universal, existing in virtually all of humanity. It crosses all cultural, religious or geographical differences. It has been true for every person of every time and place—it is a perennial truth. Such a universal human experience must be pointing to something very important about human nature and instinct, otherwise we could surely find some exception to it somewhere. But what does the primacy of human self-love teach us about our nature as human beings? Is there something wrong with this tendency that seems to exist in each one of us? Is this universal human trait a flaw in our nature, an 'original sin', something we need to somehow correct or cure? Should we see the instinctual love we have for ourselves and our primary desire for our own happiness as a 'problem' that needs solving, or could it possibly be pointing to a profound truth about us?

Wouldn't it be ironic if we spent our lives in a constant search for elusive happiness while all the time that happiness was already here within us?

Well, it is actually within each one of us. This is the great 'secret' about happiness that all the spiritual adepts of history, the true saints and mystics of all the ages and traditions, have known: happiness, which all of you are madly looking for everywhere, is actually your own essential, true nature. Happiness is not separate from who you really are at the very core of your being. Happiness is actually another name for 'you'.

If this idea is really true (which I have come to believe it is) then you clearly already know it already somehow; you may have recognized it intuitively. That's why your heart may have skipped a beat, or feelings welled up inside you, when you read about the most profound source of happiness being within. That's also why you love yourself above everything else. Deep down inside, you already know that true happiness lies within you. You know that true happiness *is* you. True happiness is innate; it is essential to who you are on the deepest level of your being. Happiness is your true nature.

Whatever is natural to the true, essential nature of a thing is always with that thing. It is considered innate to that thing precisely because it is essential to the thing's very being. The etymology of the word 'essential' comes from the Latin word, *esse*, which means 'to be'. So whatever is essential to a thing must be always present for that thing to continue to exist in being.

The chemical elements of hydrogen and oxygen, in certain very specific quantities, are essential to the existence of what we call 'water'. To be specific, water is H_2O. If neither hydrogen nor oxygen is present in these particular quantities, neither is water. If we instead have HO_3 or H_4O or H_5O_2, we may have something interesting, but we couldn't really call it water.

So our desire for our own happiness and our love for ourselves above all else is simply an essential piece of our human nature. In other words, if we are human, we have this desire—it is innate in us. Most of us don't really understand, or we fail to see clearly on a day-to-day basis, that happiness is our own essential nature. And yet we know that we simply must find this happiness we seek at all costs, so we spend most of our time and energy looking for happiness outside of ourselves. We vainly try to rearrange things around us in such a way so as to only encounter things we like, things that we believe will be possible sources of happiness. And equally, we seek to avoid or change those conditions and things that we believe cause unhappiness in our lives. It is this constant search for happiness to which many people dedicate all their energy. It produces a constant experience of craving and aversion. Yet, are all these people, places and things that we see around us every day the true sources of our happiness—or our unhappiness either?

There is a very wise and perceptive saying I once heard attributed to Marilyn Monroe, the tragic figure who never seemed to find happiness in spite of her beauty, her fame and her wealth. Marilyn said, " Once you get what you want, you don't want it."

This saying brings a little smile to our lips precisely because we have all had this same experience at one time or another. We read these words and we think: *Marilyn, how did you get to be so beautiful and so wise at the same time?* This statement by Marilyn points to the two primary reasons for a sense of misery and disappointment in your life. One is not getting what you want. The other is actually getting what you want and then realizing that you didn't really want it after all, at least not as deeply as you thought. The second cause of misery, getting what you want, is even more disillusioning than the first, because you realize that the thing you were so sure would be an answer for you isn't the answer at all. Still, this insight, though very disillusioning, can also be the beginning of great wisdom. All the people, places, things and conditions that we believe will bring us happiness come and go in our lives. After a while it becomes more and more clear to us that none of them can ever be the true source of the lasting happiness we all seek and long for. All things disappear just as they appeared, sooner or later. All things must pass. Seeing this truly is great wisdom and can be very liberating.

But right about now you may be asking yourself the following questions:

Why should I believe what he is saying about happiness not being found ultimately in any person, place or thing? Isn't that rather pessimistic? I still have hope that I will find a person, place or thing that will set me up for the future, that will finally work for me and bring permanent happiness into my life. Isn't it good to have such a hope? It certainly seems that various people, things or conditions are the sources of happiness in life. And if they are not, why do I feel so happy when I get them and so sad when I lose them?

These are all very good questions and reflect quite understandable, widely-held beliefs about the nature of happiness and unhappiness.

Actually, I am glad if you don't believe me about this. By all means, please don't believe anything you read in this book. If you believe something just because someone else says it's true, all you have (at best) is a belief in the truth and not a direct experience, a direct knowing of the truth. There is a big difference between believing something is true and knowing that it is. Jesus did not say that we should believe the truth and this belief shall make us free. No mere belief in itself can free us. He said that the truth itself will make us free. It is only in actually knowing that we experience true freedom and transformation. So it is wise to investigate any 'truth' that anyone tries to share with you. Find out for yourself what is true.

If all the people, places and things I want are really not the true sources of my happiness, why do I feel happiness (at least momentarily) when I get what I want? I would propose the following as a possibility:

Whenever you manage to obtain something you want and whenever you manage to avoid, change or get rid of something you don't want, you seem to feel happy. Understandably, you come to believe that your happiness or unhappiness is therefore based in things or conditions. When your desires are fulfilled, you have, at least, a fleeting experience of happiness. But if the happiness was really in the thing or circumstance itself, why don't you remain happy? Remember, "Once you get what you want, you don't want it." We want and want and want. We think, *Once I get this next thing I want, I'll be really happy. I'll never want anything else. I'll finally be really content.*

But has that really been our experience? Once we get what we want, do we really live happily ever after, as it says at the end of fairy tales? Do we never want anything again? Well, not really.

In reality, once we actually get what we wanted, we don't want it for very long and soon begin wanting something else. We may seem to be happy for a while with our latest acquisition, but sooner or later the happiness fades and we are back in the cycle of wanting, getting, wanting something else, getting something else. How many desires have we all fulfilled in our lifetime so far? Probably many millions. If any of them were really contributing to our happiness, surely we would be happy by now.

But why is it that after a desire is fulfilled we experience a fleeting glimpse of the happiness we seek? I think this is why: when we experience a desire for something, we also experience a kind of discontent in the mind. As long as that desire is there, our discontent continues and keeps us agitated, at least subtly. This inner discontent covers over the innate happiness and peace of our essential nature. Our true, essential nature is simply silent *presence*, simple *awareness* in the present moment, and it's always happy and content. When I fulfill a desire that is agitating my mind, the agitation ceases for a moment and, in that moment, without the agitation, I experience the innate happiness that has always been there underneath, just waiting for me to recognize it. Since my essential nature of just being present in the moment is always happy and content, when a desire is fulfilled, I realize that I am truly in the present for that fleeting moment of fulfillment and I feel that happiness and contentment. So the happiness I'm feeling is actually the simple happiness of *being* itself. When a desire is fulfilled, I stop the wanting mode for a while and in the temporary peace of mind that results the innate happiness and peace of *being*, shines forth.

This is a different way of looking at why getting what we want doesn't make us as happy as we hoped, so I'll say it again: Perfect happiness, which is our essential nature of *just being*, has actually always been present within us at the center of our very existence. But when wanting arises, whether to get or to get rid of something, our mind suffers some agitation and the agitation covers over this essential, happy nature. When a desire is fulfilled the agitation of our mind calms down and, because our inherent happiness is less obscured for a while, we feel this happiness for as long as the agitation is calmed. Therefore, even though the happiness we feel is truly always with us, we only seem to feel it when a desire is fulfilled. Naturally, we then mistakenly associate the happiness with the fulfilling of the desire. We believe it is the object we obtained that made us happy. Since we suffer from this delusion that things, situations or people outside ourselves bring us happiness, we naturally begin to think that if we can just get more and more of all these things, people and experiences, we can be happier. It's a logical conclusion, but it starts with a mistaken premise and therefore the conclusion is also mistaken.

Rather than simply enjoying the innate happiness which is always with us as the *awareness* we are, we begin to identify with all the things, situations or people we desire. All these things become 'mine'. In other words, since I am failing to realize that in my true identity as God's child, in the simple reality of just being *awareness*, I actually am already perfectly content and lack nothing, I try to enhance my personal identity by association with things, circumstances or other people that I mistakenly believe to be the sources of my happiness. This creates a very strong identification with possessions, relationships, financial status, role or work profession and public face. All this over-identification with things is simply in order to enhance my sense of a self that I believe to be somehow insufficient or lacking in something. This is the birth of the ego or false self. This false belief in lack also sets up the miserable cycle we call addiction. We end up desiring more and more of a particular thing, person, activity or substance that we mistakenly believe to be the source of our happiness. This cycle only increases our desires and by so doing keeps our mind agitated, which in turn keeps our innate happiness obscured, which makes us more discontent and prone to seek more fulfillment of desires.

You get the picture. It is a vicious circle, a never-ending cycle of craving and unhappiness. It's like the elusive carrot dangling in front of the donkey—however fast it goes forward it never catches the carrot. It's just a trick used to keep the donkey trotting on with no reward, but always hoping.

This is the way many people live their whole lives, always seeking, seeking and seeking, but never finding. Our culture seems to encourage us in this misguided pursuit of happiness. In order for us to actually discover the real happiness which lies within us, our pursuit of happiness just needs to become an intelligent pursuit. There's nothing wrong with the pursuit of happiness in itself. As we have said earlier, it is the one thing we are all looking for and is perfectly normal. We can't really give up this pursuit, until we actually uncover our authentic happiness. We simply must be happy. This deep desire for happiness is, quite clearly, the way we are hard-wired. The media exploit this natural desire that we all have for our own happiness. Turn on a TV or a radio and you will be bombarded with images and rhetoric that tries to convince you that happiness will indeed be found by fulfilling this next desire, by buying this next product, by meeting the right person on Matchup.com. We are forever looking, looking and looking for this elusive happiness, but like the carrot in front of the donkey's nose, it always seems to be just out of our reach.

It is ironic, and almost tragic, that the happiness we are seeking has been at the core of our very being all along. We are like a forgetful old man who has his reading glasses on a chain around his neck but who blunders around searching his house inside and out for the missing glasses. He doesn't realize that the very thing he seeks is with him right here and now. Of course he will never find his glasses as long as he continues the search in the wrong direction. Likewise, we will never find the happiness and well-being of union with God until we learn to look in the proper direction for it. We are looking for it out there when in reality it already exists right here and right in here. We are looking for it there and then, when in reality it always exists here and now. We are searching the world without for something that has always been within.

Jesus said, "Many looking for the kingdom of heaven will say, 'Lo it is here,' or, 'Lo it is there.' But I say to you, the kingdom of heaven is within you."

And Saint Augustine wrote a beautiful line in his

autobiographical work of *The Confessions* that sums up this situation well. He wrote, "It is for You, O God, that we seek and our hearts are restless until they rest in You."

But, you may be asking about now: *How do we pursue happiness intelligently enough to actually find it within, if it is indeed to be found within?*

I'm hoping that the following pages may at least point you in the right direction. True happiness can actually be found. It is your birthright as God's beloved child. You deserve to be happy, and my deepest hope for you is that you can stop being a seeker and begin to become a finder.

✳ CHAPTER 3

DISCOVERING WHO WE ALWAYS WERE

O God, help me to believe the truth about myself,
no matter how beautiful it is.

—*Galway Kinnell*

Ready? Are you sitting down? Because I have the most wonderful news for you. You have just won the big mega ball Cosmic Lottery to beat all earthly lotteries. You are a spiritual multi-billionaire. At the very center of your being, in your heart of hearts, you are always at peace, happy, filled with well-being and perfect contentment. You are, right here and now, already in perfect union with God. Believe it or not, you were born that way.

Another way of saying this is to say, you are God's beloved child, infinitely loved, cherished and valuable to God. There is something deep within your very being that is so sacred, so beautiful, so perfect, that even one glimpse of it could change your whole life forever and also the lives of everyone lucky enough to come into contact with you. If you already get this, you can stop reading this book right now and go out and fill the world with the joy of your radiant presence. The world needs you. You have many more important things to do than read spiritual books. However, if you don't yet quite get this but it sounds pretty good, read on. Hopefully by the time you reach the end of this little book, you will have begun to get it. I believe this was the essential spiritual teaching of Jesus. In one way or another, he was always saying: *Wake up. Realize who you really are. See for yourself that you are love, peace, joy as God's beloved children. Realize that in the very core of your being you have never really been separate from God, not even for one moment of your existence. The God of the whole universe has always been with you and in you as the very ground of your being. How much more intimate could you possibly be with God? You are already one with God in* being.

This is a radical and joyous realization that Jesus saw to be true for himself and was trying to get us to see for ourselves. He had a fire burning within him that every man, woman and child might catch his beautiful vision of the universal, holy mystery that he knew one-ness within his deepest heart. He didn't just want us to believe that he and God (the absolute reality that he saw as infinite love) were one. He wanted everyone to discover this oneness within themselves. This is an utterly transformed way of seeing reality—who I am, who you are, who God is. Even during his own human lifespan, Jesus ran into quite a bit of trouble over the radical, innovative quality of this teaching. This inno-vative revelation of God as loving father, already fully united with all his children, was probably the cause of Jesus' eventual crucifixion and death. His living out of these ideas about God and himself and everyone else he encountered, was just too different and radical for the religious conventions of his time. His teachings jeopardized the religious status quo.

Much of conventional religion, whatever the brand, is built around the idea that human beings and the sacred reality we call God are absolutely separate; humanity must, by the means the particular religion offers, work its way back to a relative state of union with God, or at least somehow appease God's 'anger'. The idea that we are already, and have always been, God's beloved children, and just need to wake up to this fact in order to experience this oneness within ourselves, can be a threatening idea to many religious people. It's especially unwelcome and unsettling for people who market religion and have a vested interest in defending the established order of their chosen creed. The idea of being separate from God, which underpins many of the doctrines, disciplines, dogmas and practices of religion, may also lead to the idea that God is quite angry at us over all the wrongs we have committed. Many religious leaders like to encourage this fear of God in order to keep people in line and preserve the status quo, even to the point of insisting on an intermediary between the common people and their God. Then this guy Jesus comes along and presents a vision of an infinitely loving God who loves everyone completely unconditionally and so he succeeds in badly upsetting many of the religious leaders of his day.

Just as we said earlier, the harmful actions we carry out, like all our actions, are motivated by one primary desire, which is our natural desire for happiness. We somehow believe that our 'sinful' actions will bring us some form of happiness; otherwise, we would never bother doing them. It is definitely true that such seeking in the wrong direction for happiness does indeed prevent us from finding it, but it is never a question of God being angry at us.

The real problem with sin is not that it makes God mad. It's simply that it just doesn't work as a strategy for finding happiness. We're quite simply looking for something (in this case, happiness) in the wrong place. Jesus understood this perfectly. That's why when people were crucifying him he knew that, in some warped logic, they believed that Jesus' death would somehow make them happy. He said, "Forgive them, they don't realize what they are doing." Jesus didn't see them as evil, just misled and confused. The God of Jesus is never angry at us or withholding himself from us. How could he when he is the very ground of our being? What have traditionally been known as 'sinful actions' do indeed prevent us from experiencing the innate happiness of union with God, but in much the same way as looking in our clothes closet for a loaf of bread would prevent us from ever finding it there. It just isn't there. The place to look for a loaf of bread is in the kitchen breadbox, possibly the refrigerator but definitely not in the clothes closet in my bedroom. If I look in the closet for the bread, no matter how thoroughly, sincerely or carefully, I'm still not going to find it. I am quite simply looking in the wrong place. The same goes for our search for happiness. If we look for it in a 'life of sin', we are never going to find the happiness we seek. Remember what Augustine wrote? "Our hearts are restless until they rest in You." Only in God is my soul ever going to be satisfied.

But don't worry; God is not a million miles away, up in some heaven somewhere in the sky or on a distant planet. God is *being* itself. He is the very ground and source of your being and mine. God therefore exists as the *I am* in the heart of each one of us. Jesus said that the kingdom of heaven is within you and it is only there that it can ever be found. In a certain sense, you yourself are the kingdom of heaven. You just fail to realize this truth.

So when people live a traditionally 'sinful' life, they are not to be condemned or judged. They need compassion. It is a tragic situation. They are looking in the wrong direction for the happiness that is their birthright as God's beloved children. It is like the ancient story from India about the princess who believed she had lost her head. She went looking all over her kingdom for the missing head until a wise old man said to her, "That which is looking is what you are looking for." So, if we ourselves are happiness, how ironic is it that we search the world over for it? We would never think of condemning or judging such a person as this princess. Nor would we think she was evil. We may think that perhaps she was insane; we would feel compassion for her and try to help.

So Jesus always responded with compassion when he encountered 'sinners'. What he often said to such people was, "Your sins are forgiven you. Go and sin no more." Of course, the religious people of his day had a lot of trouble with such a response. "How dare he! Only God himself can forgive sins," they said in outrage. But here's a novel idea: What if, by saying that our sins are forgiven, Jesus was actually saying: *Your sin is already completely forgiven?* In other words, what if Jesus was saying that God never even held one single sin against any of us to begin with? Now that is truly good news. If that is true, it would be perfectly reasonable for anyone to say at any time that our sins are forgiven. Don't misunderstand my meaning here. I am not saying that there are no consequences to our actions. There most certainly always are consequences, but I would be so bold as to say that, in Jesus' revelation of God, there is no punishment coming from God.

There is a parable that Jesus told which beautifully illustrates how the 'punishment' for sin is the sin itself, and that forgiveness is simply a matter of us changing our mind about 'sinning' as a strategy for happiness; it is never a matter of God changing his mind about whether to love us or not. Reading this parable of the lost son from the Gospel of Luke, one gets the impression that so-called 'forgiveness of sins' and the reconciliation that results is completely about a change of heart in us and never about any change in God's unconditional love and acceptance of us just as we are.

The parable of the lost son

There was once a man who had two sons. The younger said to his father, "Father, I want the inheritance that is coming to me and I want it now."

So the father divided the property between them. It wasn't long before the younger son packed his bags and left for a distant country. There, undisciplined and dissipated, he wasted everything he had. After he had gone through all his money, there was famine in that country and he began to hurt. He signed on with a certain citizen there who assigned him to his fields to watch the pigs. He was so hungry he would have eaten the corn cobs in the pigs' slop, but no one would give him any.

That brought him to his senses. He said, "All those farmhands working for my father sit down to three meals a day, and here I am starving to death. I'm going back to my father. I'll say to him, 'Father, I've sinned against God and you; I don't deserve to be called your son. Take me on as a hired hand.'" He got right up and went home to his father.

When he was still a long way off, his father saw him. His heart pounding, he ran out and embraced his son and kissed him. The son started his speech, "Father, I've sinned against God and you, I don't deserve to be called your son ever again..."

But the father wasn't listening. He was calling to the servants, "Quick! Bring a clean set of clothes and dress him. Put the family ring on his finger and sandals on his feet. Then get a grain-fed heifer and roast it. We're going to celebrate. We're going to have a wonderful time. My son is here—given up for dead and now alive. Given up for lost and now found." And they began to have a wonderful time.

All this time his older son was out in the field. When the day's work was finished he came in. As he approached the house, he heard the music and dancing. Calling over to one of the houseboys, he asked him what was going on. He told him, "Your brother came home. Your father has ordered a feast—barbecued beef—because he has him home safe and sound."

The older brother stalked off in an angry sulk and refused to join in the party. His father came out and tried to talk to him, but he wouldn't listen. The elder son said, "Look how many years I've stayed here serving you, never giving you one moment of worry or grief, but have you ever thrown a party for me and my friends? Then this son of yours, who has thrown away your money on whores and low living, shows up and you go all out with a big party."

His father said, "Son, you don't understand. You're with me all the time and everything that is mine is yours—but this is a wonderful time and we had to celebrate. This brother of yours was dead and now he's alive. He was lost and now is found."

Isn't it abundantly clear that the father in this parable never held any 'sin' against the wayward son? He didn't even seem to hear the well-rehearsed speech the prodigal had prepared about what a rotten son he had been. The father simply rejoiced that the lost son had returned. No blame, no demand for appropriate penance or restitution, no guilt trip was ever placed on the son by the father. However, the elder brother, the self-righteous, religious character in the story, was full of blame, guilt-tripping and demands for justice.

I don't think anyone would dispute that the identity of the father in the parable could represent anyone else but God. So we need to ask ourselves what this little parable tells us about Jesus' understanding of God, sin, forgiveness and unconditional love. Many of us have heard this story so many times that we fail to see just how radical most of Jesus' ideas actually are. They were absolutely shocking and unacceptable to the religious professionals of his time and, truth be told, they remain so to many of the religious professionals of our own time. I'm not saying here that sacramental confession, repentance services during Lent or good old-fashioned altar calls are not helpful or can't represent authentic turning points in people's spiritual journeys. But perhaps all these rituals and forms are more for our benefit and a deeper clarification of our own intentions, than they are for God. God seems to need no 'reconciliation' with us if we are to believe the teaching from the parable of the lost son.

At the heart of this parable is not only a teaching about our delusions concerning where true happiness lies, but also a teaching about an even more primary delusion. We don't seem to know the true identity of God, or our own true identity for that matter. Nor do we see the connection between the two. We fail to see that our true Self is inexorably linked with this absolute reality we call 'God'.

Happiness, well-being and contentment are already with us as God's beloved children and yet we wander around in a far-off country looking for these things. Our primary confusion seems to be about who we are and who God is. The center of my being (where God always dwells) is happiness itself, is always content, at peace, never troubled or anxious. It was never born, will never die, never becomes sick or grows old, is always in a state of utter joy and love and bliss. This is my most basic sense of being itself. It is the very ground of my being, my 'spirit', the most simple form of existence-consciousness that is eternally shining as the basic *awareness, I am.* This is what some spiritual or psychological traditions would call the true Self or the unconditioned Self. Jesus would probably have called it the reality of being God's beloved son or daughter. This deep sense of *presence,* or simple existence-consciousness, is not anything new that we need to acquire or achieve. That would be like acquiring your head or achieving your feet. Clearly this sense of existence is always with us because it always *is* us. It is our very sense of *being* itself. We can't lose it, we can only overlook it. And most of the time, for most of our lives, most of us do overlook it.

We certainly have many concepts and ideas about who we are, based on our countless experiences of the past and also on many constantly-changing physical or mental characteristics with which we identify. On a relative level, these various characteristics are telling us something about who we are or who we appear to be on the surface, in ordinary everyday life. Most people will probably form some opinion about who I am based on all these various characteristics. These characteristics we are speaking of here are things like age, physical appearance, gender, family background, culture or beliefs, our education or financial status. Some of these things will seem important to us or some may not seem very important at all. It depends on our psychological conditioning. This is true for my own identification with these various characteristics and also for others' impressions about who I am. For example, one person may consider my financial status to be very important. If I am wealthy that person may want to be associated with me and if I am poor that same person may not want to have anything to do with me. So all these things could be said to matter, relatively speaking, in the eyes of the world around us and even in our own eyes. But again, take the example of financial status: to one person it is the most important thing to consider in choosing a friend. To another person, your financial status may play no part at all in the opinion they form about who you are for them. They may never give your financial status so much as a moment's thought. So, all these various characteristics do seem to matter in a very relative sense only and vary from person to person.

But do they really define who you are on the absolute level? Clearly not, because since they can always change or even cease to exist, they cannot be essential to who you really are. Let's say the person we mentioned before, who doesn't like you because they don't feel you are wealthy enough, learns that you recently came into a family inheritance and now are fabulously wealthy. Their whole opinion of you would change overnight. They may even want to be closely associated with you now that you are, rich, whereas before they may have simply ignored you. But has there been any essential change in who you are, before or after your inheritance? All these changing temporal aspects of who I am on a superficial level may be relatively true of me today, but many of them will come and go in my life, or at least radically change in the course of my human life span.

But what is our true, essential being, that which remains the same through all the shifting sands of personal identity? Our true, essential being is utterly simple, present moment consciousness of *just being*, or simple existence, before we experience ourselves as existing as anything specific or particular—a woman, a man, old, young, black, white or brown, Christian, Buddhist, Jewish, atheist.

Hasn't this simple *I am* been always here, silently watching our many experiences and changing roles? It was there when we were in a little baby body gazing wordlessly out on the strange new world we suddenly found ourselves in after the quiet, dark world of our mother's womb. The same *I am* will still be silently watching through these eyes as we lie on our death-bed, and it will look around at all the familiar things in our bedroom one last time before we stop breathing and our heart stops beating. When our busy, thinking, conceptual mind that identified with all the temporal characteristics of this body quiets down a little, we can actually become conscious of this silent witness to our life, the *I am*, our most basic sense of simple *presence* here and now.

Actually living from this silent sense of simple *presence* in this eternal here and now, beyond any self-concept or personal definition is what some would call 'spiritual enlightenment' or 'awakening to the true Self'.

Jesus and many mystics would probably have called it living in the *presence of God*.

But whatever you choose to call it, it is what we are all looking for and, paradoxically, is what and who we already simply *are*. It is the very essence of who we are as God's beloved child, the unchanging core of our being. It is the *I am* within us all.

This immediate sense of *presence* in the eternal now is what we would call in the Christian spiritual tradition 'the image and likeness of God' within us. I would like to reflect on the possibility that, perhaps, Jesus was pointing to this transcendent reality within our very being in one particular aspect of his teaching. Perhaps he was trying to tell us that there is an innate divinity within us that we enjoy as God's children. I think an often misunderstood and somewhat mysterious aspect of the teachings of Jesus are the many *I am* statements of Jesus as recorded in the Gospel descriptions of his teachings: "I am the bread of life, I am the light, I am the way, the truth and the life. I am the resurrection. Before Abraham was, I am."

These *I am* statements are strongly reminiscent of the *I am* statement that God himself is recorded as having made to Moses in Exodus 3 by way of a kind of divine self-definition or name. When Moses asked God who it was that had sent and commissioned him with a message to Israel, God said to Moses, "Tell them that *I am* has sent you... I am that *I am*." In light of these well-known *I am* statements of God to Moses, it probably seemed grandiose of Jesus to be making the same statements about himself, at least to the well-indoctrinated religious people of his time. But what did Jesus intend by this frequent use of the phrase *I am* ... followed by very open-ended nouns that had a kind of transcendent flavor to them, such as light, life, resurrection? Was Jesus making a specific reference to the subsequent theological development of an exclusive or unique divinity for himself alone?

This seems unlikely, since we would be hard-pressed to find any implication from Jesus' own words directly claiming that he was different from, or superior to, any other person or somehow exclusively related to God. In fact, we find several instances where he seemed to be saying just the opposite:

"Why do you call me good when only God is good?"

"I can do nothing of myself, it is the Father who does the works within me."

"The works that I do, you will do and even greater works will you do."

What can we make of these words attributed to Jesus himself? In light of the fact that many Christians have often put Jesus on a very exclusive pedestal, claiming him to be the one and only Son of God, these words can sometimes confuse us.

We must willingly admit that the teachings of Jesus were not handed down to us in a series of clear prose writings from his own hand. He left no writings himself. Following an extensive oral tradition, during which the teachings of Jesus were passed down by memory for several generations, they were written down in a somewhat terse style in what would have to be called fragments. In reality, we have some parables and a sermon. These are the recorded 'teachings of Jesus' that are available to us today. There are some even more enigmatic sayings attributed to Jesus that can be found in some early Gnostic Christian manuscripts. And even though these writings were subsequently condemned by the early orthodox interpreters, they may give us some further clues as to what the actual teachings of Jesus may have been. We really don't have an absolutely clear idea of what the real teachings of Jesus were. However, when a phrase or theme appears frequently in the extant documents we do have, it seems safe to say that it is very probable that Jesus actually used the phrase or theme himself.

So what about this frequent use of the *I am* theme? Surely Jesus was aware of the famous *I am* statement in reference to God found in Exodus 3. So his intention seems to probably have had something to do with connecting his own *I am* with the *I am* of God. But in doing this, was he making reference to an exclusive divinity for himself alone, or was it a teaching on a principle pertaining to humanity in general? Is the *I am* that Jesus speaks about his own, exclusive *I am* as the unique incarnation of God, or is he speaking about the, *I am* that exists in each one of us as well? Could this *I am* phrase be an expression of Jesus' own discovery of the innate divinity that exists in all human beings alike as God's beloved children?

I must admit that sometimes I feel that we have been misled concerning the actual teachings of Jesus by our strong focus on the idea of his exclusive divinity. This concept that Jesus had an exclusive role as the only incarnation of God, the only *I am* with a human body, reflects the subsequent development of Christian thought and theology which took place gradually many years after the actual 'Jesus event' happened. We have, perhaps, overlooked the possibility that, in his teachings, Jesus himself may have been more focused on the divinity within us all as God's beloved children, rather than on an exclusive divinity dwelling in himself alone. Or do we really think that Jesus' revelation of God as

Abba (father) was all about an exclusive relationship between God and himself alone? He said several times, in effect, *You can do all that I have done and even greater things if you experience the union and oneness with God that I do.*

Is this the statement of someone who saw himself as being in a special or exclusive relationship to God? He didn't seem to go around making special claims for himself, but appeared rather to be saying that we all have the possibility of realizing that we all are what he is, a son or daughter of God. Could all these *I am* statements of Jesus therefore be pointing to a teaching on our own innate divinity and a missing link between our own *I am* and the *I am* of God?

Perhaps Jesus was actually trying to tell us this: *If you come to the realization of your own basic unity with the infinite being of God, just as I have; if you learn to consciously identify yourself with your own innate divinity found in the I am that dwells in the heart of each one of you, you will discover your true identity as God's children, just as I have. Then you will be able to be what I am and do the things I have done. And you may even conceivably do greater things than I have done.*

And what 'things' did Jesus do? Well, let's see: he healed all kinds of illness and disease, gave sight to those born blind, 'cleansed' lepers, walked on water, calmed storms with a word, multiplied food and raised dead people back to life. Even if you posit that some of these stories may be exaggerated, it seems reasonable to think that not all of it could be. Even if only two of these accounts are true, it's still pretty impressive—don't you think?

If this possibility of doing 'greater things' than even Jesus did seems incredible to you, remember,

Jesus also said, "The kingdom of heaven is within you." What did he mean by that? The implication seems to point to the idea that something absolutely divine and sacred, the kingdom of heaven no less, dwells somehow within each of us already. If this is true, there may be truly amazing, untapped abilities in any human.

Jesus' revelation was that God is our loving father-mother. Yet we sometimes seem to forget that to speak of God as our parent says, something not only about the nature of God, but about our own nature as well.

Perhaps Jesus' unique revelation in the history of religion is not only a revelation of God to humanity, but also a revelation of humanity to itself.

If God is our Father-Mother, what does that make us? It seems to be a metaphor that implies that the absolute reality of God is the very source of our own being. If we were brought up in a Christian family, we may well have been conditioned through our early years to believe in and accept the divinity of Jesus. As beautiful as this traditional teaching of the divine incarnation of Jesus is, was this his primary message to us? What about the idea of a divine incarnation in each one of us? Was this what Jesus was actually pointing to? Even though orthodox Christian theology and all the ancient creedal statements state that Jesus was both human and divine, do most traditional Christian churches or believers really believe or teach the idea that Jesus was actually human in any way that we could actually relate to our own ordinary, human experience? Could it be that the teachings of Jesus were trying to point his hearers in a direction of their own identity as essentially divine, as God's beloved children?

I have come to feel that his teachings were actually

much more radical and innovative than most of us would ever dare to imagine. His teachings may be calling us not only to believe in the Christ in Jesus alone, but to believe in and live from the Christ within all of us as well. I truly believe that this was Jesus' dream for us all, that we might awaken to the truth of our own divinity as God's beloved children and so discover the secret of true happiness within our very being.

"O Father, may they be able to live in our oneness as I am in you and you are in me. May they be one in us." Jesus prayed this for you and for me. Your own spiritual awakening will be the answer to this prayer of his, prayed so long ago for you.

CHAPTER 4

NOW *I* AM

*A woman wore a necklace round her neck but forgot it
was there. She began to search for it and made enquiries.
A friend of hers, realizing what the woman was looking
for, pointed out the necklace round the seeker's neck. She
felt it with her hands and was happy again. But I ask
you, did the woman get the necklace anew? Ignorance
caused her grief and knowledge her happiness. The
necklace was never lost or gained anew. Similarly in
the case of the one seeking the Self, there is nothing to
be gained anew. Ignorance of the Self is the cause of
the present misery, knowledge of the Self will bring the
sought for happiness.*

Sri Ramana Maharshi

The search for personal identity can ironically seem
quite complicated at times. Frequently one hears
about the young son or daughter of an acquaintance
who has quit college at about the half-way point.
Having left everything they own in their parents' base-
ment, they take a year off and leave for Europe or even
India, to 'find themselves', say their parent. Indeed it is
a peculiar search to try to 'find oneself'—is it not? Isn't
it a bit like the story of the princess who went searching for her head? When one sets out to find oneself,
who is it that seeks and who is eventually found? Are

there two selves? Wouldn't you think that who we really are would be entirely self-evident? What could be simpler than to find oneself? After all, if you are seeking yourself, you don't have far to look.

This reminds me of a story of the Sufi mystic and spiritual teacher, Mullah Nasrudin. Nasrudin goes into a bank to cash a check and the bank teller says, "Excuse me, but I'm going to need some ID, sir." The Mullah takes a little mirror out of his pocket, looks in the mirror for a second and says, "Yup, that's me alright."

Yet somehow, we find that finding ourselves is not always so easy, is it?

The saints and mystics of the various traditions would all tell us that discovering who we are is so simple and so clear that we often miss it. Have you ever been looking in a well-stocked grocery aisle for some small item like, say, a jar of black olives, and somehow you manage to look right past it when it is right in front of your face? I know I have done this very thing many times. We do this with our true identity of *awareness*, which is always present. Perhaps the problem lies in the fact that we live so much of our lives up in our heads, stuck in a world of concepts and ideas about who we are, while we ignore our own most direct and simple experience of it. For is it really ever possible to actually *be* anything or anyone other than just who I am?

If we learn to pay close attention to our own simple, everyday direct experience of just *being*, who we are will become quite obvious, self-evident, as plain as the nose on your face. In this very moment, in any moment, your own most direct experience of who you are is really very simple: you are simply a field of conscious, choiceless *awareness* in this present moment, here and now.

It's true that you are probably engaging in some activity or other in this present moment. For example, right now you are reading these words on this page. What you are doing in the present moment is constantly going to be changing. You may set aside this book and take a drink of water, eat something, or go answer the phone. But whatever you happen to be doing, the most basic sense of existence is always about *being*. *Being* is always the very simple reality of your conscious *awareness* in this present moment. The 'doing' of the present moment is always obviously secondary to simply *being*. Now I am reading; now I am taking a drink of water; now I am eating something; now I am talking on the phone. What is the one common factor in every one of these statements? Isn't it the *now I am*? The *now I am* precedes any particular doing. The *now I am* is the substratum, the most basic underlying reality that makes possible all the varied, ever-changing human experiences or doings. Before we are anything else—a man, a woman, old, young, well or sick—we are a human being. So, there you go. The mystery is solved. Who you are is *being* itself, simple *awareness* in the here and now.

Again, this is so obvious that we somehow overlook it. We miss the forest for the trees. We are often so focused on the 'doing' in this moment that we miss the *being* that underlies it. We simply don't notice the substratum, the background of simple *awareness* that is always the truest, most basic sense of who we are. It is the essential aspect of who we are—this *now I am*. It is essential because it is the one thing about me that is always present and never changes. This background of simple *awareness* that is ever-present, is my true Self for which I may have been searching everywhere. Like the head of the princess, it was always here. Where else could it possibly be?

So who I am, on the most basic and fundamental level, is this ever-present, unchanging *now I am*. The *now I am* in me is the absolute in me. It is absolute because it is eternally ever-present, immutable, unchanging. Sri Ramana Maharshi called this *now I am*, the Self. He described it as 'self-shining'. Its very nature is to radiate, just like the sun. And what it radiates is *awareness*, love, joy, peace, well-being and happiness. When we come to a sense of awakening to this deepest, most essential dimension of who we really are, we have tapped into all the love, joy, peace, well-being and happiness we have been looking for somewhere out there.

This innermost center of our being that we are talking about here has been called by many names: the inner light, the Self, the true Self, the image and likeness of God, the indwelling Christ, or Buddha nature—to name a few. But whatever you call this reality is less important than your actual experience of it—or rather your awakening to your experience of it—which is actually always present.

Sometimes people on a 'spiritual journey' hear these various names and terms referring to our authentic, deepest identity and they form a kind of spiritual concept that they come to believe in, rather than actually experience. They come to think of their true Self or spirit as a kind of ghost in the machine, an invisible entity that inhabits their body. Even if you believe quite deeply in this entity and believe it is who you are on the deepest level, you may still not be actually consciously experiencing it as anything more than just another concept about who you are, albeit a very 'spiritual' concept.

True awakening is always about direct, actual experience, not just an intellectual experience of yet another concept. It is so easy, and deeply ingrained in us to make even the most profound and potentially transformative spiritual truth into just another concept to believe in, rather than an actual reality that we live. We have been conditioned throughout our lives to do this with anything and everything, often even more so in the realm of religion and spirituality. Religious formation or education often has a strong element of learning a list of beliefs that one is required to subscribe to intellectually, in much the same way as one would learn a list of dates and historical facts while taking a course on world history. The lists we learn and memorize in such a religious education are made up of such things as various concepts about the nature of God, outer ritual and personal comportment expected in church or temple services, religious customs and practices.

All these things may have their place, but they are simply the outer shell of any religious faith. They often have little or nothing to do with the transforming inner experience that should be the essence of all true religion. All the religious paths of the world were founded on the direct spiritual insights of an inspired founder or founders. In order for a religious path to remain vital and alive, the main focus must be on a direct experience of these inspired insights in the actual lives of the followers of the religion. Living spiritual experience is absolutely crucial. Otherwise religion simply becomes just another ideology, a set of concepts or beliefs in the head that the religious adherent feels compelled to defend as the correct view about reality, God, the world or the human soul. There have always been adherents of the various religions who seem almost exclusively focused on all these outer shell aspects of religion, while ignoring, or at least de-emphasizing, the inner core of actual spiritual insight and experience. This phenomenon is what is responsible for the post-modern tendency to divide religion from spirituality.

We frequently hear a person describe themselves as *spiritual but not religious*. Many people have grown weary of lifeless religion that simply requires sub-scribing to a list of beliefs about God and a certain commitment to attendance at services and financial support. To just continue believing what their parents and grandparents happened to believe has ceased to be meaningful or desirable for many people. They want to have a deep, personal experience of spiritual truth that directly affects their life. That is to say, they are seeking the actual transformation of consciousness that all reli-gion claims to be about. So the important point to any spiritual path has to do with actual, direct experience and not just more concepts and beliefs, or dry knowl-edge learned by rote—no matter how lofty or spiritual such concepts, beliefs and knowledge may seem.

The experience of just *being*, what we are referring to here as *now I am*, is actually the most direct and pri-mal experience of everyone already. Our sense of *now I am* is actually always present underneath the surface consciousness of people, places, things and ideas. It is eternally present now, can never be lost and is not separate from what we may call an experience of the sacred. Everyone is looking for this experience that is paradoxically not an experience at all, but rather, is the ground of all the possible human experiences we could think of. This being the case, why does our conscious *awareness* seem so rare, elusive, esoteric or difficult to attain? Probably because it is not something we can ever attain or know as just another object, by learning facts about it, having beliefs or concepts about it or even by reading about it in a book like this one.

If this book has any value at all for you, it is only as something pointing to your actual experience of this reality we're talking about here. It's like the old Zen saying about a finger pointing at the moon. The reason for a finger pointing at the moon is for someone to actually look at the moon. Just focusing on the finger serves no purpose. The pointing finger isn't about the finger, it's about the moon. Once the moon is seen, the finger becomes secondary. All religious and spiritual concepts and teachings are like the finger pointing. We cannot know the Self, the *now I am*, by studying words about it, we can only actually know our true Self by *being* it. This sounds simple because we can never be anything else. The reason it does not seem so simple for most of us is because it is not about forming more concepts and beliefs—and forming concepts and beliefs is what we humans seem to do rather well. Since we are all so conditioned to live most of our lives in our head, which is to say, lost in a complicated, purely conceptual veil through which we see everything, we are somewhat puzzled, bewildered and bemused by a reality that is so entirely concrete, so wholly ontological and existential.

So how do we learn, on a practical level, to go against this habitual focus on the conceptual and consciously experience the liberation of *now I am*? How do we learn to simply *be*? The various spiritual traditions have developed various spiritual practices and I will present a few practices here. They are not particularly original or innovative. I am simply going to attempt to strip down the practices that have worked for me to their most basic essence, hoping that one or two of these practices may make sense to you and be of some benefit as pointers to reality. In essence, each of the practices you will hear about in this book is really one and the same. You can know the Self (which is not separate from the sacred reality of God) only by *being* that Self. So all the pointers to the Self which follow are pointing toward the experience of just *being*—to the *awareness* that we are all actually already experiencing all the time.

The eternal here and now is the first pointer. It should be an accessible pointer for everyone since—guess what?—it is always *now* and you are always here. You have no choice in the matter. Who you essentially always are is the *now I am*. Whatever the means adopted to wake us up to this fact, we must all at last return to our essential Self, to the reality of *now I am*, if we are ever to discover the innate happiness we have been talking about in this book. So, since it is always now and you are always here, why don't you simply abide in the *now I am*—right now? It sounds simple, right? Why does living in this simple consciousness that is always with us, seem so complicated?

As we said earlier, we are often stuck in a purely conceptual world. We all have so many concepts, beliefs and opinions about God, ourselves, others, the world and reality in general. Most people take all these concepts quite seriously. They believe that their concepts about reality are actual reality. They believe that their concepts about God *are* God. They believe that what they think about themselves and others is actually who they really are. This is the basic human dysfunction. We have all created a personal little self, others, a world, a god—in fact everything—out of a bundle of thoughts and concepts and beliefs about reality, and then we believe that this conceptual construct is real. But can the mystery we call life ever be reduced to a bunch of concepts, beliefs and opinions?

Now

One very widespread concept about the nature of reality that almost every human being on the planet believes in wholeheartedly is the concept of time. But it is important to see for ourselves that time, which seems so real to us, is entirely conceptual. We exist in the eternal here and now as simple present-moment *awareness*, as *now I am*. There is simply no disputing this fact. If we could get out of our head for a minute or two we would see for ourselves that *now I am* is always the only concrete, direct experience which underlies *all* possible human experiences. It is the only reality we ever have. The past, with which I so often identify is utterly gone now. It is merely a concept a memory of what was actually experienced as a now. The future is an entirely imaginary concept, of what we believe may or may not happen. But in reality, the only direct, real experience any of us ever has is, here and now. Isn't this entirely obvious when you really look at it? Past and future are always only concepts. We can never directly experience either one except as a thought in the now. Just because past and future are merely concepts, that is not to say they are not useful ones. We can certainly use the concept of time to plan practical matters like vacations, doctor's appointments, or retirement parties. Of course we can. There is no problem with that. But most of us make the concept of time into a problem by constantly reacting emotionally and psychologically to the past and future so strongly, so much of the time, that we are just barely aware of here and now, the only real time we ever have.

Since the *now* is the only time that ever actually exists, it could be called, the absolute reality. Past and future are real in one sense only. They each have a relative reality borrowed, so to speak, from the actual, living reality of here and now. Past and future only exist relative to the *now*. Past, present and future, the three times, really only exist as the one eternal *now*. They are all only *now* in actual, non-conceptual reality.

Just as the present moment, *now*, is the central actual existing point in the concept we call time, so the present place, here, is the actual existing point in the conceptual sense we call space. Here and now are the points in space and time, actually the same *one* point, in which we all experience our own most basic sense of being.

Here and now, I am.
In this here and now, I have absolutely no past
and no future

This may all sound rather philosophical, esoteric or abstract, but if you really look at it, it is anything but abstract. It is entirely concrete and experiential, not abstract or theoretical.

You can't really know this truth concerning the eternal *now* as only an intellectual or philosophical concept. You have to awaken to it existentially. As I communicate these words to you about the eternal *now*, I am communicating from my own direct awakening to this reality. If these words resonate within your being, it is because you are awakening to this reality yourself. Otherwise this would all seem rather meaningless to you (which it undoubtedly will to some). True awakening is caught, not taught. On a very deep level of your being, you already know the truth of the eternal *now* of God, because that is who you really are already. Once you have had even a glimpse of the eternal *now*, you have the possibility of learning to drop the habitual human tendency to focus on an imaginary past and future and begin to dwell in the eternal *now* of God's presence. You are beginning to awaken to reality. This is the most liberating experience. You can live in peace and joy in this eternal *now*.

Of course, the mental habits of a lifetime may have a certain momentum that continues propelling us for a while. If you are in a car going 50 miles per hour and you suddenly turn off the engine, the car will still make a forward motion for a little while before it stops. You may not experience a sudden and complete falling away of the concepts of past and future—yet. Or maybe you will. There is no rule in this regard.

But if you even have had a little glimpse of the *now*, you can never be the same again. You have seen a truth that is truly liberating and transforming. Even if you find yourself falling back into a conceptual trap of past/future focus out of pure habit, simply remind yourself of the little glimpse of *now* and re-enter eternity. Please be patient with yourself and realize that when you catch yourself not being present—you are present in that instant of catching yourself. In fact, the experience of being present and the experience of not being present are both experiences arising in this present moment. Whether you feel aware or not aware, there is always someone who is knowing this. Who is the knower who knows whether you are feeling present or not present? Can't you see that this knower, this *awareness*, is eternally present and aware? Otherwise, how would you ever even know the experience of not being present?

So you can't really ever escape *presence*, whether you happen to feel present or not. Think about it: can you ever really not be present? How could you possibly be more present or more aware? Trying to be more present is like trying to exist more. If you try really hard, could you exist more than you do already? Remember, you already are pure, clear *awareness* in this present moment. No matter what experience you are having, no matter what thoughts you are having about that experience, there is always a present-moment *awareness* of the experiencer, the knower. And the name of this knower is *I am*.

You are that *I am*.

CHAPTER 5

LIVING THE AWAKENED LIFE

There is a story in the life of the Buddha that soon after his enlightenment he was living the life of an itinerant teacher, and a young man who encountered him was so impressed by the radiance of the Buddha's presence that he thought he must be someone very special. He asked the Buddha: "Sir, are you a great and wealthy person or some kind of king?" The Buddha replied: "No." Then the young man asked the Buddha: "Sir, are you an angel or a demon?" Again, the Buddha replied, "No." Running out of possible guesses as to who, in fact, this radiant being appearing before him might be, the young man finally asked the Buddha: "Sir, are you some kind of god who has taken on a human form in order to teach people the path to enlightenment?" And once again, the Buddha replied: "No." By this time the young man was very mystified and decided to take a more direct approach. He simply asked the Buddha: "Sir, please, tell me who or what you are. For I know that there is something quite different between you and other men I have met." And then the Buddha looked kindly into the eyes of the young man and simply said: "I am awake."

The concept or ideal of awakening or enlightenment has been made to seem quite rare, difficult or esoteric, but the reality of it (which has nothing to do with concepts or ideals) is quite simple and always effortlessly present here and now. Enlightenment is awakening from the dream of a false, conceptual sense of self. In other words, you are not who you think you are. But to take this a step further, you have to renounce the idea 'I am enlightened'. When you are able to cut through even that idea about yourself, you will truly be enlightened and will have dissolved attachment to any identification. Then you are free. If you think you are 'enlightened' you have to always be careful to act like an 'enlightened person'. Behaving like your concept of an enlightened person will lead to... more concepts, not to awakening.

You are quite simply who you are right now in this very instant, nothing more, nothing less. So, what do I mean by this? Let's investigate this statement a little. Who or what are you? What is your actual experience of existing right now in this instant? What is your most direct, essential experience of basic consciousness?

To use simple grammatical terms we learned as children, we could say that who you are right now in this moment, is the first-person singular, present tense of the verb to be. What simple phrase do you see if you look at the first person, singular, present tense of the verb to be on a grammatical chart? You see the simple phrase, *I am*. There is a well-known spiritual practice known as 'self-inquiry, which we will look at in depth in the next chapter. The essence of self-inquiry is simply to investigate this *I am*. It is not an intellectual process or the repetition of a question about who you are in a mantra-like fashion. It is more a matter of intuitively asking oneself: *What is this eternally present* now *that is constantly shining as this conscious sense of* am-ness *that I always effortlessly, naturally experience right now?*

In other words: *Who am I?*

In self-inquiry there is a simple resting in the first person, *I*, and the present tense, *now*. We investigate calmly, pay attention and focus peacefully. This type of investigation into who you actually are in your direct experience of simple *being* is not at all difficult, complicated or esoteric. How could it be? It is simply a conscious looking at who you already, effortlessly are. Can you ever not exist? Can you not be present?

An enlightened person is simply someone who is consciously aware of this, that's all. Your enlightened Self is this simple *I am* that is always eternally, peacefully present. How then can it ever be not present or be something special that you must attain? Enlightenment is always here and now. Seeking enlightenment is exactly like the deluded princess we met earlier in this book who went looking for her lost head. You can travel the whole world looking for your head and you will never find it because it is sitting on top of your body. You can only find your head when you stop looking for it and simply realize that what is looking for your head is indeed the very head you have been looking for. So, enlightenment is the very simple, ever-present *awareness* that has been seeking enlightenment. You will discover enlightenment in the very moment you simply learn to rest in that ever-present, effortless consciousness of *I am*. Nothing could be more simple than this.

This being the case, can you see how enlightenment, in the most absolute sense, doesn't really even exist at all as anything other than a concept? We think that enlightenment is some kind of rarified, special state that a few people living in caves in the Himalayas have maybe attained. Yet, it is actually the simple background of *awareness* that is present everywhere in absolutely everything and everyone who exists. The joke, as they say, is on you. True enlightenment is not a state of consciousness at all. It is the simple *awareness* in which every single state appears and disappears. It is simple *being* itself. You are now, and always have been, the consciousness, *I am*. Nothing can ever change that fact, nor is it possible for you to ever be anything else. The big cosmic joke that put the little smile on the lips of the Buddha is this: *Enlightenment is the realization that you and everyone else are already enlightened.*

We all think that enlightenment is the final goal. But realizing this truth of enlightenment is just a beginning. Once we realize the truth of who we are, we need to integrate this truth into our everyday, ordinary lives. True awakening has very clear implications for ordinary life. We have almost all lived large portions of our life believing (if we have questioned it at all) that who we are is nothing more than a conceptual self, based on roles, relationships, physical appearance and other such characteristics. For a long time I thought that I had a past and future and so lived in alternating states of hope and fear. When we totally believe in our conceptual sense of self, we live in our heads, we identify quite seriously with all the roles, relationships and functions that we play in life. Don't get me wrong here, I just finished saying that enlightenment will inevitably affect our everyday lifestyle and choices. All these things, roles, relationships, activities do matter on a relative level and have a certain validity in our everyday lives. But, in the most absolute sense, none of these things can ever define the essential, eternal *I am* that I have come to realize as my true identity. The *I am* can never be defined, but realizing it certainly has an impact on many things that can be defined. All the relative realities of my life do matter, but only on that relative level; they are never absolutely important. One can quite naturally see how realizing this truth might simplify life and make it less of a deadly serious affair.

It's a lot like an actor playing a role in a play. The role I play in a stage production of *Fiddler on the Roof* is not really who I am, is it? Let's say I am playing the role of Tevye. In my role I am a Jewish father of five daughters in Russia at the turn of the last century. If I am a good actor, I will have learned my lines, rehearsed my songs and know my cues. I hope that people will enjoy my portrayal of Tevye, so I will say the lines as they were written, I will sing the songs I am supposed to sing when I am supposed to sing them and I will try to be convincing and really feel my part as fully as I can. Tevye is not who I really am but, on a relative level, when I am on stage during a performance, I become Tevye for the audience. Just because I am not Tevye in any ultimate sense in real life, that doesn't mean I can go out on stage and sing the 'Star-Spangled Banner'. Well, I could do that, but if I did I couldn't really expect to get very good reviews from the theatre critics. So I play my role in a totally appropriate way, as it was written, and I fully enjoy the experience of playing the part of Tevye. I hope the audience will enjoy my performance. But when I go home that night, or even during the course of the actual performance, I am not going to be conflicted and angry about my daughter in the play marrying a gentile or the possibility of my family being displaced to Siberia. Because I am sane, I realize that ultimately these happenings are simply part of the

story and I don't get truly upset by them. Even though
I am playing the role of Tevye, I'm not going to take
the various happenings in his life personally.

✓ Does this mean I don't take my role seriously? No.
I take it relatively seriously as a role, but I don't take it
absolutely seriously because, on an absolute level, it is
not who I really am. So it is when you come to realize
who you are on an absolute level in real life. You still
play certain roles, you take these roles seriously as far
as they go. You try to play your role well. Just because
I realize who I truly am, that does not mean the role I
play in the relative world doesn't matter. Of course it
matters, relatively speaking. Realizing who I really am
on the absolute level actually can assist me in moving
through the relative level of reality much more skill-
fully and competently. When we really come to realize
who we are on an absolute level, when we see that we
are the spacious *awareness* in which all relative realities
appear and disappear, we enjoy a stability and a peace
that remain unshakable.

This is not to say that, after a profound awakening, we will never again experience sadness, anger
or upset of some kind or another. Of course we will.
These experiences are simply a part of the normal
human scene. Awakening does not mean that we stop
experiencing the full range of normal human emotions.
It just means that from an absolute, enlightened perspective, I no longer feel compelled to take such emotions so personally. I realize that they are not really
personal at all. They can come and go as much as they
like and my true Self, which is simple present-moment
awareness, is untouched by them, just as the screen in
a movie theatre is untouched by what appears on it.
After awakening we experience all the normal human

emotions—sometimes even more intensely than before. This is so because we are more able and willing to allow whatever may be arising in each moment, even the most unpleasant, difficult emotions. The open, spacious *awareness* that you are is so open and so spacious that it can contain whatever arises in it, no matter how uncomfortable or unpleasant it might seem. In fact, you begin to see that whatever is arising in this spacious *awareness* is not at all separate from the very space itself in which it arises. You become one with the spacious *awareness* and one with all that comes and goes within it. Life ceases to be a problem and you begin to just sit back and enjoy the ride. Have you ever been on a really good roller coaster at an amusement park? In a three star roller coaster there are some great, dramatic hills and drops. After all, it wouldn't be much fun or very interesting otherwise. And then of course you need some level parts of the ride in order to fully enjoy the more dramatic parts. It all has its place. It is all just part of the ride. You learn to appreciate all of it.

As I mentioned earlier, this simple *awareness* that is always present is by no means just within you. It is within all that exists as its basic unchanging essence. It's not merely 'within': it is the very nature of existence itself. When you begin to see this clearly, you simultaneously come to understand that you are not at all separate from anything whatsoever. Just as you can look at your big toe and, in a certain sense, think of it as an individual entity, you also understand that it's not really a separate entity at all, but is simply a part of your body. Your big toe is, in a certain sense, in your body just as much as your body is in your big toe. They are separate and yet one at the same time. Likewise, every single thing that exists is actually just existence itself. All the seemingly separate people and things that surround you, as well as you yourself, are simply an expression of existence or *being* itself. There is in reality no separation to be found anywhere.

Certain implications naturally follow from the clear seeing of this truth. Would you go to the tool shed behind your house, take out a hammer and begin pounding your big toe with it? I would hope not. Likewise, when you see the innate oneness of all that is and understand the interconnectedness of reality, you can never consciously cause harm again to any person, place or thing. You become always kind and compassionate to anything and anyone you encounter. Why? For the same reason you are kind to your big toe. Because you *are* your big toe and your big toe *is* you. Being kind to your big toe is not profound sanctity or virtue. It is simply sanity. You are within all of life and all of life is within you. Once you see this clearly, you always act accordingly. There's no big mystery in this, is there?

The awakened life comes with a very natural sense of contentment and happiness. It is the happiness of *being* itself and has always been with you. The awakened life is an awakening from the dream of suffering. The real cause of suffering is not to be found in any particular negative experience. Suffering is found in the belief we have about the experience or the story we tell ourselves about it. Suffering is the story we tell ourselves: *this should not be happening right now.* When we actually realize that who we are is open, spacious *awareness* in this present moment, we understand that we can accommodate absolutely anything that arises in this moment. Nothing at all is ever unacceptable to *awareness* any more than any event happening in a room would be unacceptable to the space in the room. A baby could be born in the room in the morning and then, in the evening, someone could be murdered in the room. The space in the room in which both of these events unfold never objects to either event. You could take a basket of fragrant, colorful flower petals and throw them all over the room, or you could take a bucket of black mud and animal excrement and toss it all around the room. Yet the space in the room would remain untouched by either. This is certainly not to say that the birth of a baby and a murder are the same. It is just pointing to the absolutely spacious *awareness* in which every single event that ever happens appears and disappears.

This analogy is pointing to the stability and unconditional peace that is your own true nature of pristine *awareness*. This stability and peace is never absent or disturbed, no matter what is happening. It is entirely unconditioned. When you consciously realize this presence of the stable, open *awareness* which is always present, you yourself are a center of peace and tranquility in the midst of a world that often seems anything but peaceful or tranquil. You become one of the peacemakers that Jesus called blessed. You live in an open *awareness* which is spacious enough to hold tenderly anything that life gives: living or dying, joy or sorrow. A thousand joys and a thousand sorrows will come and go, but the spacious *awareness* in which they come and go will remain forever the same.

Thinking and the mind

Certainly, thinking is a big part of the ordinary human experience—we have thousands of thoughts every day. Thinking is a wonderful function of the

human brain that can be a very useful tool for carrying out many everyday, practical objectives like
solving a mathematical problem, baking a cake, doing
your income tax return or balancing your checkbook.
All these daily activities involve the functional and
necessary use of the human brain. There is clearly
no problem with any of this. The problem with most
people's relationship to thinking is that it goes much
further than this ordinary, functional use of thought.
The thinking function can quite simply be used as a
tool in a practical way and then put away, just like you
would put away a hammer or some other tool after use.

However, many of us have been pretty much
incapable of ever putting this particular tool back in
its box. Instead, there is a constant engagement with
thoughts in the form of judgments, opinions, beliefs
and concepts. With that engagement come belief and
personal identification with the content and the process of the thoughts and, without realizing it, we have
created an imaginary entity that we call the mind.
We believe that we are this mind, which is merely a
bundle of thoughts and memories. In believing that we
are these thoughts and memories, we effectively cover
over our most basic and fundamental sense of identity,
which is pure *awareness* in this present moment. "You
are the veil that hides the paradise you seek," said Saint
Brendan, the fifth century Irish monk.

Awareness is the true paradise you seek, the one
source of joy, peace and stability. This simple sense of
presence in the eternal *now* of God is really who we are.
It is our true Self; the *I am* which is our innate, joyous
sense of direct, felt oneness with *being*, with God. The
imaginary entity called the mind is the thin veil that
hides it.

But instead of simply being just who we are, being the happy, beloved child of God in this eternal *now* of God, we tend to create this false imposter of a self that manifests as the voice in our head which offers a running commentary on everything. In many people's experience, this voice in the head never shuts up. It is almost like some kind of annoying sports commentator on television who is commentating non-stop and distracts you from simply enjoying the game. This voice seems to be incessantly judging, evaluating, complaining, plotting and, quite often, simply whining. By believing in this unceasing inner commentary, we obscure our own true, radiant being, or *presence*.

The way to short-circuit the tendency to create this imaginary entity, which we sometimes call mind or ego, is not to simply decide to quit thinking, in the same way that we might decide to quit smoking or cracking our knuckles. Intentionally trying to quit thinking is a lot like telling someone not to think of pink elephants. If you intentionally make a goal out of not thinking of pink elephants what happens? Of course you can't seem to think of anything else but pink elephants. Likewise, if you make a spiritual goal of not thinking, the voice in the head only becomes louder and more insistent. All that is necessary to restore a more healthy relationship with this thinking function is simply to learn to notice the spacious *awareness* that is always already present. Be aware of the one who is silently listening to the little voice in the head. The head-voice, you will discover, constantly changes, comes and goes. The silent listener to the voice always remains, just quietly aware. This, silent listener is who you really are, not the relentlessly commentating voice in the head.

Once you realize this, you see that there is really

no need to continue creating this burdensome sense of a little self. When you realize who you really are, the voice can continue its commentary, and probably will do so for a while, but there has been a major shift of emphasis. Now you are no longer identified with it, you can see clearly that you are not the voice and the voice is not you. When there is no longer any identification with all those thoughts, they begin to slow down, quiet down, and eventually subside for the most part. Believing so fervently in all these thoughts is what gives them life, so to speak. Once you clearly see that they are not you, but only thoughts, they will come and go like clouds in the sky. Just as you sometimes make the observation, "Oh, it's a cloudy day today!", so you will notice when a lot of thoughts are present or when not many thoughts are present. Neither the presence of thoughts nor the absence of thoughts are important to the spacious *awareness* that is conscious of their absence or presence.

I believe this truth about the non-existence of an actual entity called 'the mind' is what many *jnanis* or respected self-realized teachers from India are referring to when they talk about the death of the mind or ego-death in some of their teachings. It's not saying that an enlightened person becomes some kind of blubbering idiot incapable of speech or rational discourse. I believe that what some of these teachers may be trying to say is that there is no actual entity called 'mind' that exists at all in the first place. Just like there is no such thing as the boogey man, Santa Claus, the Easter bunny or unicorns and jackalopes. At least none of these things exist literally as far as I know.

So the death of the mind that teachers like Sri Ramana Maharshi or Sri Nisargadatta speak of, is a kind of figure of speech or a verbal shorthand. If there is no mind-entity to begin with, how can it really die? It's like the snake in the rope metaphor we use in the next chapter on spiritual practice. If you think you see a coiled up snake in the corner of your garage in the dim light of evening, and you look at it long enough to discern that what you thought was a snake is actually a coiled up rope you placed there last fall, did you manage to kill the snake? Well, you might say that but it wouldn't be accurate. You can't kill a snake that never existed. So likewise, it's not really a matter of the mind dying. For an awakened person, the mind is dead because it simply never existed.

This leads us to another truth about how it is 'after' awakening: there is also no separate doer either. If there is no actual, separate, little entity around, if the mind and ego are just fleeting thoughts that appear and disappear on the screen of *being*, then who is left to do anything? After awakening (if the word 'after' is appropriate for the eternal present) a person clearly sees they are not this little, imaginary, finite entity called mind or ego—it is only the Self or God or *being* that is the doer. For them, it is God who is doing everything. For them, life just lives itself in this eternal *now*. There are no separate little doers who are calling their own shots. After awakening, this is clearly seen, while people who haven't yet realized their awakened Self still have a sense that they, personally, are doing, thinking, planning and executing.

The Self/God/*being* alone exists and does everything. Life just keeps living itself and takes care of everything. This is true for even the most seemingly insignificant things, like walking across a room or taking a drink of water, as well as the seemingly more momentous happenings, like leaving home and moving across country or changing jobs or getting married. The Self/God/*being* does everything, absolutely everything, with no exception. So life just flows through us, life lives us and we are not separate from life. It's like the well-known saying in the writings of Saint Paul found in the New Testament, "It is no longer I who live, but Christ lives in me."

The person living in that Christ consciousness sees all other human beings as the Christ and treats them accordingly. The Christ consciousness lives through that person, so they become free from neurotic projections and emotional addictions and can live in the present. They don't mistake people's conditioning for who they really are. They come to see everyone as 'original innocence' rather than 'original sin'.

Terms such as 'awakened', 'self-realized' or 'enlightened' are merely figures of speech to enable us to talk about all this, but are not really a true or accurate way of expressing it. Absolutely speaking, there is no such thing as an enlightened person. A so-called 'enlightened person' is simply one who has seen through the common belief in a separate little mind or ego as an actually existing entity. An enlightened person is one who has awakened to the direct knowledge that all that really exists is the Self/God/*being*. There is, in the absolute sense, no such thing as a person, let alone an enlightened or unenlightened person. It's like saying there are two types of unicorns: curly-haired unicorns and straight-haired unicorns.

Even so, it may be helpful to say that there is really no need to adopt a bunch of eccentric ways of speaking after awakening. Language can only point poorly to something entirely beyond itself. If we get too caught up in having it somehow accurately reflect the absolute reality (which it never can), we kind of miss the point of the pointing. Some people adopt their own non-dualistic language: they avoid certain ordinary ways of speaking, like the use of personal names, reference to persons at all, let alone any reference to enlightened or unenlightened persons, or the use of any personal pronouns. These dualistic grammatical transgressions are seen as quite serious offences—almost what we used to call, in my own spiritual tradition, mortal sins. Perhaps they are trying to use this new way of speaking as a kind of teaching tool in order to shock people into an awakening.

Again, it is much like the example of playing a role in a play or stage production of some kind. If you play a role in a stage production you may refer to yourself as George or John or Tallulah while you are on stage and you may have a professional stage name in addition to the name of the character you are playing. Performers are quite aware that these various names are not really their own, but using them is simply an aspect of being a performer. When you are a character in a play, you may refer to your son or wife or husband in the play, but you are always well aware that these relationships are not real in the way most people think of such relationships. If you got up on stage and insisted on constantly reminding your audience that your name in the play is not actually your real name or that your wife in the play is actually married to someone else, you would probably succeed in ruining the play and annoying everyone involved.

So just because we have had a profound awakening or are enlightened or liberated, that is no reason to go around being difficult or fancy about the way other people choose to speak. We ourselves can just speak normally, while being aware that we are simply using conventions of speech that are not really true on any absolute level. Simple and straightforward language, to point towards the holy mystery beyond words that is simply *being*. This was the approach of many wonderful, respected teachers like Sri Ramana and, if it was good enough for him, it is good enough for me.

Waking, dreaming, dreamless sleep and the 'fourth state'

Most people, enlightened, or not yet aware that they are enlightened, seem to experience at least some semblance of present-moment *awareness* in the normal waking state. Many of us would say that, in the waking state, we are conscious in our experience, at least partially and most of the time. But then people go to sleep and, if asked, they would say that they are not conscious in that state. Yet we can wake someone up from sleep by calling their name or making a loud noise, so there is clearly some semblance of consciousness.

Then there is what we call the dream state. When they are dreaming most people believe fully in the dream world where they find themselves. If a rabid dog is chasing you in your dream, you generally believe this is happening while you are dreaming. If you win the lottery in your dream and become a dream millionaire, it seems very real to you while you are dreaming it. But some people experience what we call lucid dreaming. They dream like everyone else, but in their dreams (or in some of their dreams) they are aware that it is all only a dream situation. This is an interesting phenomenon in light of the actual enlightenment experience in waking life. It's like a little preview of awareness in the midst of everyday life in which we realize on one level that it's all just a dream and that things are not really what they seem. Like lucid dreamers, awakening means that we continue to live in the relative dream world of everyday, conventional life in the waking world, but we are fully aware as we do so. This lucidity greatly changes the experience of life in both cases: whether it is in the sleeping dream world inhabited by lucid dreamers, or the waking dream world that we find ourselves moving through 'after' awakening.

We have made a brief exploration of the worlds of dream, sleep and waking consciousness, which absolutely all human beings seem to experience, whether they are enlightened or not yet aware of it. But 'after' awakening, how do we experience these three universal human states of consciousness we call wakefulness, dreaming or dreamless sleep? Is there a different experience of these states and, if it really is different, then how is it different?

After awakening, no matter what particular state we are in we are always conscious that we are *awareness*. All of us, at all times, are already pure *awareness*. There is simply no doubt at all about this. However, after awakening we, and indeed anyone whom we call awakened or enlightened, always have a direct, felt experience that reflects this ever-present, pure *awareness* that we all are. This being the case, we remain consciously aware in the middle of any state, whether waking, dreaming, or even in deep sleep.

This is the paradox that comes from the limitations of language which we have already discussed: it's not always helpful to create a conceptual division about the difference between living the awakened life and living a life where we do not know our true nature.

Nevertheless, there is a difference and it becomes clear when we investigate the three common states of human consciousness.

Living the awakened life, even in the midst of deep, dreamless sleep, there is a direct, felt experience of the reality of conscious *awareness*; there is an awareness of sleeping. I have jokingly called this 'lucid sleeping'. In the awakened life, there is often less need for sleep and I suspect that this may be because there is so much less energy invested in carrying the burden of maintaining and catering to the imaginary entity we call the mind or ego. Even though this mind-entity is a non-entity without substance or discrete existence, when we still believe in its existence it takes quite a bit of our physical and psychological energy to keep it going.

In the teaching of Ramana Maharshi and others, there is mention of a fourth state beyond the states of waking, dreaming or deep, dreamless sleep. This fourth state, or *turiya*, is in reality, not a state at all, but is rather an idea or teaching that points to the one reality of the pure, clear *awareness* in which all the three states of waking, dreaming and deep sleep come and go. The awakened person is always abiding in this state that is not really a state at all. States come and go, but this *awareness* that is our true nature has no comings or goings. It is immutable, birthless, deathless. All appears and disappears within it. It alone remains. This is living the awakened life.

CHAPTER 6

SPIRITUAL PRACTICES

The practice of the Presence of God, though a bit painful in the beginning, if practiced faithfully, works secretly in the soul and produces marvelous effects and draws to it in abundance the graces of the Lord and leads it insensibly to the simple gaze, that loving sight of God everywhere present.

—Brother Lawrence of the Resurrection, seventeenth century monk

In my own spiritual journey I have developed for myself a practice of prayer I call the prayer of *simple being*. It is, as the name suggests, a very simple form of what you could call contemplative prayer. This prayer form actually arose out of my study of the teaching on prayer I found in a book called *The Cloud of Unknowing*, by an unknown English mystic of the fourteenth century, and out of my practice of 'centering prayer' which I learned during my formation as a Trappist monk at the Abbey of Gethsemani.

Spiritual practices are a kind of practice for real life. The best spiritual practices are simply pointing to who you are already. The idea behind a spiritual practice is to help you discover the truth about who you are, who God is, and that in fact these two are not separate realities. Perhaps this very simple prayer form may assist you in living more consciously in the eternal here and now in your normal, everyday life, and so help you to uncover the innate happiness and peace of your own true nature as God's beloved child. I hope so. There are just two basic guidelines for what I am calling 'the prayer of simple being':

The prayer of simple being

Guideline One: At the beginning of your prayer, sit in a posture you find comfortable and meaningful, (just sitting on a chair is fine). Sit silently for several minutes, letting go of any thoughts or concerns that may arise. Relax into the silence of just sitting. After a few minutes of silently just sitting there, focus on God dwelling within your heart as the very ground of your being, in the simple consciousness, *now I am*. This is your most basic, primary sense of simple *presence*, which is the silent awareness of just being. This simple sense of being present now is not separate from the *presence of God* within you. Simply, silently turn your focus on this *awareness* alone. Rest in this *awareness*. There's nowhere to go, nothing to do. Right now you are simply *being* in God's presence. You cannot be anywhere other than in the *presence of God*. Peacefully abide in this very simple sense of just being in a silent interior gaze of love for God dwelling within you as that *I am* which is always present.

Guideline Two: If during the course of your prayer any thoughts about anything whatsoever arise in the mind, simply and very gently drop the thoughts and return to the silence of just *being*. We define thoughts here as any words forming in the mind. Language is something you acquired as you grew up. However, there was a time in your life, very early on, when you had no language. During this prayer you have decided to lay down the tool of language you have acquired. Verbal language is not necessary in this prayer. Instead you are using the language of *silence*, which is really the language of love. The basic idea is to remain in the consciousness of just *being*, very simply and silently. Rest in this silent *awareness*, abide in this thought-free state of just *being* as fully as possible and let the mind rest. If thoughts begin to form in the mind, gently drop them and return to the word-free silence of *being*. Just be here and now in love, wordlessly, with God dwelling in your heart as *I am*.

If you like, you can take this simple prayer form and use it each morning and evening as a way of bringing more conscious presence into your life. Remember, your most simple sense of *presence* in the here and now is not really separate from God's presence. The *I am* is the very *presence of God* itself at the center of your being. It is the divine indwelling, the ground of being of each one of us. So, when you are simply present in this way, you actually are yourself, the very *presence of God*.

If you like, you can start with the two daily prayer times using this prayer of simple *being* for about twenty minutes each time you pray. Use it as a way of anchoring yourself in this most basic and deepest sense of identity and *presence*. Eventually you will notice a greater peace and tranquility arising in the rest of your daily life, even in the midst of situations and experiences that may have upset you in the past. If you persevere in this practice you will begin to notice a certain slowing down of the frenetic activity of your thinking. Your daily life will begin to quiet down and the constant inner commentary in your head will become less compelling. The commentating head-voice may still be there from time to time, but you will take it a little less seriously.

Gradually, it will begin to dawn on you that who you have always been, on the very deepest level, is simply this silent *awareness* of just *being*, thought-free, free of concepts about life and more simply present to life itself. This is actually your most natural state—just a quiet, alert sense of *presence* in the eternal *now* of God. You will have begun to learn the secret of the perennial spiritual quest: to 'pray without ceasing'. In this eternal *now* of God, with no past and no future, you come to realize that life is simple and filled with joy, the simple joy of being, immersed in God's holy presence. Your personal problems begin to fall away one by one. After all, what problem can continue to exist in the eternal *now* of God? In order to have problems you need a past and a future. In the eternal *now* of God's presence, which is not separate from your own simple sense of *presence* right here, right now, there are no problems at all. There may well be situations that call for a response of some kind, but you no longer feel the need to label them as problems. When such situations arise, it will be clear to you what can be done in that moment. You will feel an inspiration to act (or maybe not to act). If you are inspired to act, you will do so in peace, knowing that ultimately, as Julian of Norwich said, "All shall be well, all shall be well and all manner of things shall be well."

Self-surrender

Another simple practice that is a pointer toward the experience of just *being* is the practice of self-surrender. Self-surrender is basically to let go of any inner resistance to whatever arises in the eternal now. Surrender flows out of a basic sense of trust about the unfolding of your life experience. We know, as Julian of Norwich said, that all is well in the absolute sense of things because we know that ultimately God is in control of the unfolding of the universe. As you learn to surrender, you learn to let go of judgment, complaints and inner resistance. You learn to stop fighting with reality and you give up the rather futile goal of having everyone and everything conform to your will. This is why this practice is called *self*-surrender. You are surrendering the little, petty sense of self that always demands its own way no matter what. It is that limited sense of self that says: *My way, or the highway.* You no longer feel the need to demand that life always come out on your own personal terms. Self-surrender teaches you to just be in the present moment, with neither judgment nor agenda. It teaches you to live more fully in the simple consciousness of *now I am.* The *now I am* is simply present, it never judges, criticizes or interiorly resists *what is.* It is totally surrendered in the *now.* It accepts this moment just as it is.

The practice of self-surrender is often misunderstood; it is not an idealistic concept which leads to an utterly passive life or the avoidance of any decisive action. Of course we can always act and are sometimes even obligated to do so. Self-surrender is always about offering no inner resistance to *what is.* Again, it does not mean that you can never do anything to help change a situation. Working for change is not at all incompatible with the practice of self-surrender. In certain situations it may even seem quite obvious to you that working to change something is the only compassionate and responsible thing to do. But in the state

of self-surrender, *as* you act, you are also in a place
of inner emotional acceptance that: *Yes, this situation
is the way it is right now.* There is no longer an inner
argument with reality going on. There is no longer any
inner resistance to *what is*, though there may well be
some form of outer resistance that may be completely
appropriate to the situation as needed and deemed
necessary. The basic stance of surrender is to accept
fully, then act as appropriate. And acting can take the
form of either concrete, physical action, or affirmative
prayer of petition. In my experience both can change
situations if practiced diligently.

The foundation of self-surrender is rooted in the
understanding of the four traditional theological attri-
butes of God's being that we know as all-knowing,
all-powerful, all-loving and all-present. Because God
is all-knowing and all-present, nothing can happen in
the universe without his knowledge. Because God is
all-powerful, nothing happens without his permission.
And finally, and perhaps most importantly, because
God is all-loving, nothing happens that, in some way
or other, is not ultimately for the greater good of all
concerned. In our limited, human perception of things
this may not seem readily apparent to us in a particular
situation, but that does not make it any less true. This
may sound like a dualistic, conceptual 'idea' of a distant God from whom we are separate—we are super-
imposing these words onto the infinite, unchanging
Self/God/*being* which alone exists and acts within and
through all beings and is the ground of our own being.
Until profound awakening, until we see our own Self
and our own *being* radiating the love and acceptance
that we are—then let us rest in and surrender to that,
whatever name we may give it.

In some non-Christian traditions this same teaching may be sometimes seen as an impersonal law of karma, cause and effect, but in essence it is the same practice of learning to trust the unfolding of life as it happens and letting go of all inner resistance to *what is* in this moment.

However, changing the lifetime habit of inner resistance to reality may quite likely require a good deal of practice. But once you begin to experience the peace of mind that results from this self-surrender, it becomes easier and easier. There are several wonderful resulting fruits that gradually ripen and manifest in your life from the practice of self-surrender. More love, joy and peace flow into your daily experience. In general, life becomes lighter and easier to deal with. Challenging circumstances will definitely still arise in your life from time to time. This is simply part and parcel of the basic human experience and always will be. However, such challenges will not feel so overwhelming anymore. You begin to see yourself as the beloved child of God—as Jesus saw himself. When challenges and difficulties come, instead of fretting and fuming, you find yourself saying within: *This is not my problem, but is God's. My Father is taking care of this.* Jesus taught that, unless we become as a little child, we cannot enter the kingdom of heaven. Self-surrender helps us manifest the charming and wonderful characteristics that we love in little children: transparency, freedom, innocence, joy, trust and, yes, even fun. And as little children seem to attract people wherever they go, we will begin to attract the people around us as well. When we begin to smile at the world, the world tends to smile back.

Self-Investigation

One who mistakes a rope for a snake is cast into fear thereby and his fear and distress can be removed only by knowing that it is a rope. A friend who knows this tells him so and he then investigates for himself and finds it to be so. There is no other way.

Likewise, he who seeks liberation through knowledge of the True Self must investigate into the Self with the help of someone who has already realized the Self, who being free from desires, is a knower of God and an ocean of grace.

Sri Ramana Maharshi

There is an ancient Indian analogy that illustrates well how we can be mistaken about our perceptions of things. Sometimes we really think we are seeing one thing but it turns out, when we investigate the thing a little further, that the reality is not how it appeared to us at first glance.

This analogy is called the snake in the rope. A man was in, let's say, the garage of his house. It was right at dusk so the light in the garage was dim. There were so many things in his garage. He was thinking as he looked around: *I have got to find the time to clean this garage out.* Just then he looked into the corner of the garage and saw a large brown snake coiled up, with the upper part of its body standing up like it was ready to strike. Startled, he jumped back and, as he did so, his back brushed the wall and turned on the light. To his relief he saw that the snake was actually an old rope he had used last year that was rolled up sitting in the corner of the garage. He turned the light off and went back in the house, relieved that there was no big brown snake living in his garage.

The saints and mystics of the ages tell us that this is pretty much the way many of us view reality in general. We often see something that isn't there at all and fail to see what is really there. Since we seem to have collectively forgotten our true identity as God's beloved children, we miss seeing the innate happiness, security and joy that are our essential nature. So the first snake we see is when we look at ourselves. The mystics and saints of all traditions would tell you, *You are not what you appear to be. There is something within you, at the core of your being that is infinitely more vast, beautiful and awesome than you could ever imagine. You are love. You are security, you are pure joy and peace and abundance. All those things, those experiences, those states for which you expend so much energy searching, are as close as your next breath. Wake up and see!*

But should we just take these people's word for it? I have said countless times in this little book: "Your true nature is happiness and peace and love and joy." But if you don't see this for yourself, I can say it until I am blue in the face and it's not going to be of much help to you. So, while I myself have no doubt that you are the beloved child of God, infinitely loved, beautiful beyond description, pure love, joy, peace and happiness, you need to see this for yourself. This is the whole point of what we call spiritual practice. Such practices are there to help you see for yourself the true nature of God, yourself, and the world around you. Remember, Jesus said "You shall know the truth and it will set you free." He didn't tell us to *believe* the truth and it will set us free. So, just like a scientist with a rigorous approach to truth, it is important for us to conduct our own experiments with the truth and come to verify for ourselves just what the truth actually is, by experiencing it for ourselves. Spiritual practices are just such experiments.

A spiritual practice from the eastern tradition of India that is frequently called 'self-inquiry', which we have looked at briefly earlier in this book, is one such spiritual experiment that we can use and that can help verify the truth of who we are on the very deepest level. I prefer to call this practice self-investigation, because I believe the word investigation is more descriptive than the word inquiry in describing this practice.

If you walked into your garage this evening and thought you saw a big brown snake coiled up in the corner ready to bite you, you might do one of several things. You could run screaming from the garage. This is a pretty safe option. At least the snake wouldn't have much opportunity to bite you if you ran out right away. However, your spouse would probably laugh at you when you both went back to see the snake, turned on the lights, and discovered an old rope instead. Another option, if you had a hard time believing that a snake would actually be living in your garage, would be to take a closer look at the snake, to investigate it. At first, just in case it was actually a snake, you might stand perfectly still, squint your eyes a bit and only visually investigate more closely. If your eyesight was fairly good and the memory of putting the rope in that corner of the garage last September came back to you, it might not even be necessary to turn on the light in order to discern what was what. If, after looking closely at the snake you still had doubts about what you were actually seeing, you might grab the old hockey stick propped up against the wall next to you and poke a little at the snake. After a few such pokes you might think, *well the snake is dead.* You then might get closer and actually see that your snake is really a rope. You get the idea.

If you see something that you believe is actually there and is dangerous, but you're not quite sure, you look more closely at it, you poke it, you investigate it any way you safely can, and you try to verify for yourself what it is you are actually seeing. The practice of self-investigation is like that. In self-investigation one scrutinizes, or looks directly at, their most basic, primary experience of the Self which, as we have said already, is the basic consciousness, *now I am*. It is attending to this most basic experience of simple *being*, scrutinizing it, until the reality of just what this inner core of your being actually is in reality, begins to dawn on you. It's a lot like looking very closely and carefully at the snake in your garage until the truth dawns on you: *Oh, it's just a rope. It's not a snake at all.*

Now this practice of self-investigation is sometimes seen as an advanced practice. This is not to say that there is anything particularly esoteric or difficult about it, though. It's just like taking Spanish courses in school. When I was in high school, I took Spanish and later, in college, French. If you have ever taken a language course or, for that matter, any kind of subject like math, history or philosophy, you know that courses need to be taken in the proper order if you are to learn the subject as effectively as possible.

First, you take Spanish I then Spanish II; maybe you stick with it and eventually take III or IV. It helps when you take an advanced Spanish course to have gotten the prerequisites to the course out of the way first. They were necessary in earlier courses in order to lay a foundation in your study of Spanish. The advanced Spanish course uses the language tools you acquired in the first, second and third courses to take you to a new advanced grasp of the Spanish language. If you have no

Spanish grammar, vocabulary or spelling under your belt, it's probably not very effective to be taking an advanced Spanish course.

So, in order to practice self-investigation effectively, it helps to have a calm demeanor. You can develop an interior quiet from meditating, doing mindfulness practices, taking up silent prayer or watching the breath. Any basic contemplative spiritual practice can help calm the mind and sharpen attention, which are the prerequisites necessary to effectively practicing self-investigation. It also helps if you have had some insight already into the eternal here and now that we have previously mentioned. Remember, in self-investigation practice you are investigating the consciousness, *now I am*. In order to investigate something you need to see it first. In order to figure out that the snake in your garage is actually a rope, you need first to have laid your eyes on it.

But if you have actually had a little 'aha' moment around this idea of the eternal here and now, even if it was somewhat fleeting and you returned to your ordinary perception of linear time composed of a past, present and future, you have completed a course entitled *Who I Really Am: Level I*. You have acquired a little tool you can use to take a new course entitled *Who I Really Am: Level II*.

Take your insight about the here and now and just sit quietly with it. You saw, at least for a brief moment, the truth about *now* being the only time we ever have. This is not something you come to see with the intellect only, although it might seem like it. You come to see the truth of the eternal *now* by actually experiencing it. Again, this is a little 'aha' moment, like a light bulb lighting up in your mind. It is like the little 'aha' the man had with the snake in his garage: *Oh yeah, I put that rope there last September. That's not a snake at all; it just looks like one in the dim light.* That's what happened with you and the eternal *now*. You suddenly saw the truth of the situation. Once you really see something, even if briefly, you can never really look at it in the way you used to, at least not completely.

So take this experience of the eternal *now* and sit quietly with it. Let it soak into your consciousness. Really allow yourself to feel it, yes. All there ever is, is *now*. Right now is the only direct experience I ever have—ever. You don't have to think these particular words in your head—just let yourself be immersed, so to speak, in the simple consciousness of this eternal *now*, in this very moment of your experience.

After several minutes of soaking in this awareness of the *now*, shift your attention slightly and be aware of the simple consciousness of your own basic beingness, the *now I am*. Become aware that the sense of *now I am* is also always immediate. That's why I say *now I am* and not just *I am*. *I was* or *I will be* are concepts without substance in the *now*. The consciousness *I am* is always *now*. The only true and direct experience of *I am* is always, eternally in the *now*.

When you let your consciousness soak a bit in the awareness of *now I am*, you begin to actually see that the *now* and the *I am* are one and the same reality. Who is aware of the *now*? It is *I* who am aware of the *now*. When am I aware of the *now*? Well, now of course. So, *now I am* are not two. Who you really are, on the very deepest level, on the most basic level, is the *now* itself.

You are never separate from the *now*. The *now* is eternally with you. It is essential to you. You are the *now*. And the *now* is you. Sit quietly and just experience this in your deepest being. If your mind begins to wander into other things, questions, thoughts about lunch, tomorrow, next year, just quietly repeat to yourself again the little phrase, *now I am,* and just rest in that awareness. Use the little phrase, *now I am* like a hovering sea gull uses a brief flap of the wings to keep itself afloat in the air.

Have you ever watched sea gulls glide around on a beach coast? They glide, seemingly without effort and let the wind keep them in the sky. But every now and then, they find themselves losing altitude and they briefly flap their wings, just enough to keep them up in the air. That's the way to use the little phrase, *now I am.* Just use it very gently, quietly, and then rest in the *awareness* it points to. Another little pointer phrase you can use that works in the same way and incorporates this insight that, in reality, you are the *now,* is the sentence: *What is this eternal now, ever shining as the awareness, I am?*

You follow the same directions with this little question. It is just another little wing flap that keeps you gliding in the bright blue sky of *awareness.* You are investigating the *now I am.* You are practicing self-investigation or self-inquiry.

The wing flap isn't the point. It is just a means to an end. It keeps you up in the air of *awareness.* Just rest in the *awareness,* not the words themselves. You don't repeat the phrases like some kind of mantra. They are only little pointers. They point you in the direction of pure *awareness,* but the *awareness* itself is what you rest in, abide in, investigate. Peacefully investigate the consciousness *now I am,* and see what you discover for yourself about yourself. When you do this repeatedly and persevere in it each day throughout the day, it begins to dawn on you that your true identity is, in fact, the *now*. You have a direct experience of the fact that who you really are, is just simple, pure *awareness*, ever present, ever peaceful, ever happy and content. You begin to wake up and see the real you, the real nature of reality itself.

CHAPTER 7

BUT HOW DO I JUST BECOME 'MORE AWARE'?

Since I have begun to attempt to share with others some of the truth discovered about *awareness*, who we really are, who God is and where our true happiness lies, I am often asked the question that makes up the title of this chapter: *but how can I just become more aware?*

All the spiritual practices I have shared with you so far are simply little pointers to the direct, conscious experience of the spacious *awareness*, which could be called your true Self, union with God, or simply, the *presence of God*. But spiritual practices are a bit like a bunch of different hats on display in a department store window. In such a display window you might see a wide variety of different hats. One hat might be very colorful with lots of feathers in it. Another hat could be a simple, brown stocking cap. You might see a classical English derby that an English stockbroker might once have worn in the City of London, and next to it you might find a cowboy hat that a Texan would wear to the neighborhood barbecue. But whatever the hat looks like, whatever its style, all hats are really serving the same purpose. A hat is mostly worn to protect your head from sun or rain and possibly to keep your head warmer in cold weather and, of course, there are certain social implications too. The important thing about picking out a hat is to find one that fits you and that suits you, to find one that you like.

All spiritual practices are meant to point to the presence of pure, spacious *awareness*, which is not separate from what some would call the *presence of God*. Some spiritual practices do a good job of pointing and some do not. In this chapter I would like to strip down, to its bare essentials, what I have come to feel is the true essence of all spiritual practices. What I am about to describe to you is, in my opinion, the most basic, functional, simple hat in the display window of spiritual practices. If none of the other practices I have described seemed to appeal to you, I hope the following approach may be of some benefit.

In actual fact, the question *How do I just become more aware?* indicates a basic misunderstanding about the true nature of *awareness* and a basic misconception about the true nature of reality. For some reason, we just seem spontaneously to see reality as being divided up into innumerable, separate objects. In this mistaken perception of reality, we often see ourselves as just another individual object in this vast sea of objects. We think that, on our own, we are not whole or complete, and we imagine that one or more of these objects we see all around us might do the trick for us. At first, most of us focus pretty exclusively on material objects. But when we begin to wear out this belief that some kind of material thing is going to bring fulfillment or happiness, we may begin to go after more subtle objects that have a spiritual dimension to them. Some of us may have let go of the idea that winning the lottery would do it for us, but we may still think that enlightenment probably would.

The problem is that, for most spiritually inclined folks, enlightenment is always some far off, future attainment that seems a million miles and a million years away. For many, *awareness* is just such an elusive attainment that they must strive to somehow realize in the future. But the truth I have been trying to convey throughout this entire book is that it is actually quite impossible for you to ever become more aware. *Awareness* is not a skill that you now lack and must somehow acquire through a lot of difficult effort and practice, like learning how to play tennis, the piano or backgammon. The *awareness* you are so earnestly seeking, is actually who you already are. This being the case, how could it not be always, perfectly present?

Even if your conscious, felt experience right now is that you have been hopelessly non-aware for the last two hours, there is still someone to whom the experience of non-awareness is happening. That someone is *awareness*. There is someone who is, ironically, aware of being non-aware. So, because *awareness* is simply who you always are, you can never not be aware because you can never not be you. Every thought, perception and experience is always appearing and disappearing in this pure *awareness* that is you. It doesn't really matter whether you think of yourself as an evolved, enlightened person or a distracted, unaware person. However you may see yourself, it is ultimately simply a concept about you that is appearing and disappearing within the space of *awareness*.

So this background of *awareness* is who you are on the most absolute level precisely because it never, ever goes away. All the other stuff with which you identify, which you think of as being you—your age, your physical body and appearance, your occupation, education, financial status—it all eventually goes away. So, if any of it was really you, in any absolute sense, who are you once all this stuff is gone? Can you see how none of it could possibly be you in any absolute sense? That pure, crystal clear *awareness* that so many of you may be so earnestly seeking, is the very consciousness that is aware of your seeking. So all you really have to do (which is really not a doing at all) is relax and notice the presence of this *awareness* which is already within you. Try to slightly shift your attention in the midst of any and every experience and, rather than being exclusively focused on the experience alone, notice that which is aware of the experience while it is happening. It's really quite easy; you just need to get the hang of it.

At various times in my own spiritual journey, as I shared in the introduction, I managed to stumble into this presence of pure *awareness*. I loved it and was always concerned with how I might be able to sustain it in my everyday life, but I misunderstood the true nature of this *awareness* almost entirely. I was convinced that it was an ability or skill I lacked somehow and that I could cultivate in my life by doing something. So, I did something. I strained and put forth a tremendous effort to be mindful. I went on numerous intensive, silent retreats and a lot of the time even carried the practices I learned on these retreats into my daily life as much as I could. They weren't always the kind of stuff that really translates well into normal, everyday life, even life in a Trappist monastery. I purposely slowed down all my movements, tried to live in almost total silence, and I mentally noted every activity I was doing while I was doing it. I probably silently said to myself many thousands of times; *walking, walking, eating, eating, breathing, breathing, thinking, thinking.*

Now I'm not saying at all that such practice was entirely useless. But I was doing all these things in order to acquire an *awareness* that I believed was outside my own experience in that moment. In actual fact, none of the thinking, eating, walking, breathing, none of it at all, could have possibly even existed outside of this backdrop of simple, natural *awareness*. The *awareness* I was looking to attain had never left me, I just didn't see it.

It is important for us to realize this very clearly if we want to live a life that is truly aware. No experience could possibly exist without this *awareness*, just as we have discussed elsewhere in this book, no object in a room could possibly exist without space in the room. Physical space is a metaphor for *awareness* that many spiritual teachers have used as a little pointer to this reality.

So, noticing the *awareness* that is always, already here is not a matter of acquiring anything at all. It is simply a matter of shifting attention slightly, just as you might decide to shift your attention from the objects appearing in a room to the space around the objects, or you might shift your attention from focusing on a movie appearing on a movie screen and begin to notice the presence of the screen itself.

On the next page there are two illustrations that are simple examples showing how we can shift our attention and see something in a completely different way.

The first illustration is a drawing of a cube.

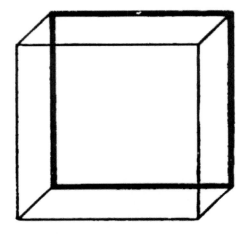

fig. 1

As you look at this cube, notice that there is one side of the cube that is drawn darker than the other sides of the cube. First look at the cube and think of this darker, outlined side as being the front of the cube. Now shift your focus a little and think of the same darker outlined side of the cube as being in the back of the cube. Now just go back and forth in your perception. Now the outlined side is the front of the cube, now it's the back, now the front, now the back. Just keep shifting back and forth. Can you see how you can change your whole experience of the cube by just slightly changing how you are focusing and what you are focusing on?

The second illustration is a drawing of a woman. Some people look at this drawing and see a young, beautiful woman in semi-profile with a very large hat on and with long, luxurious blonde hair. Others look at this drawing and see an old hag with a big hook nose and shoulder length white hair. Which woman can you see? Can you see both, or only one? If you can only see one, just keep looking at it. You will probably eventually see both women.

fig. 2

These illustrations simply illustrate how the *way* we look at something can make all the difference. I hope they give you some simple sense of what it might be like to experience the radical perceptual shift that we sometimes call enlightenment or awakening.

Some people spontaneously experience such a radical shift in their perception of reality; suddenly and dramatically they notice the presence of pure *awareness* in which all things are always appearing and disappearing, where before they merely noticed objects that are appearing and disappearing. But not everyone's experience of the shift is dramatic, sudden or even complete. For others, the realization that pure *awareness* is always present as their own true nature is more like a gradual blossoming that slowly flowers within in progressively deeper ways.

Some flowers, like the famous night-blooming cactus, bloom dramatically all at once in a matter of seconds. One minute there is a dark green, closed bud then, in the next second, there is a beautiful flower bursting with color. A few similar flowers do exist, but it seems that such sudden blooming is somewhat rare in the world of nature. Most flowers bloom in a much more gradual manner. You notice that the plant has formed buds in the spring time. The buds may stay for several days and then begin changing color quite gradually. Then the buds begin to slowly open, perhaps over a day or so. Then one afternoon you pass the plant and it is in full, glorious bloom.

One flower is not superior to another. They each bloom in their own way. There is nothing anyone can do to make a flower bloom to order. The flower will bloom when it's good and ready, as long as it has sufficient water and sunlight. If you feel that you are not blooming 'spiritually' speaking, it will happen eventually, I promise you—just like the bud that unfolds into blossom as part of the rhythm of the great dance of life.

You can actually use even the experience of not being aware to take you to *awareness*. Here's how:

The next time you are feeling very unaware, unspiritual, or like a fundamental spiritual failure at this *awareness* business, quietly turn your attention to the presence that is aware of the frustration, that which is aware of the sense of being a failure. Just gently turn your attention to the one who knows the experience of failure. This knower is always present, no matter what is being experienced in any given moment. Otherwise you would not even be aware at all of the experience of being a failure at being aware. The experience of being a failure is arising in that pure, perfect *awareness* that you feel you lack as a spiritual failure. By believing the story of yourself as a spiritual failure, you are effectively covering over and blinding yourself to the *awareness* that can't help but always be there. Remember our little fish friend who was searching for the ocean at the beginning of this book? Or what about the princess searching for her lost head? We laugh at these characters in the stories, but are we really so different?

Or to return to the space in a room metaphor: imagine you are spending an afternoon shopping for antiques with a friend. You see an antique armchair in a shop that you fall in love with and, on impulse, you decide to buy it. The next day the chair is delivered to your house and you realize that your living room is already pretty much filled up with other furniture. There is seemingly no space for the armchair. What to do? Do you bring more space into the room from outside? No, that's not really possible. Instead, you simply take a few things out of the living room and suddenly the space for the arm chair appears. Did you have to go to an expensive space store and, at great cost to yourself, purchase more space for your chair? No? Likewise, all the *awareness* you need is always right here and now. If you can drop the story that is crowding out your experience of *awareness*, you will suddenly realize that you are already aware. In fact even that is not quite accurate. You will not realize that you are already aware; you will realize that you are *awareness* itself. If *awareness* itself is who you are, some special doing or intense effort is not really necessary, is it?

On the relative, human level, you will continually experience many thoughts, perceptions, situations.

This will go on for your entire life in this body and will never stop. Some of these experiences will seem very spiritual and some will not, but whatever experience you are having must be, and can only be, experienced in the vast, empty space of ever present *awareness*. Every single form that exists must exist in this emptiness. Forms need emptiness to exist and, in a certain sense, we could even say that emptiness needs forms to exist. If there was just a vast empty space, with no forms existing within it, then the emptiness could not be said to exist in any way we could really appreciate or perceive. We could never experience emptiness without form, nor could we ever experience any form without emptiness. That's why the relative and absolute aspects of reality are never seen as contradictory or incompatible once there has been a profound awakening.. The absolute and the relative are like two sides of the same coin. They are not two at all.

Therefore, every single thing that appears in your experience, with absolutely no exception, is a form that can't help but point toward the emptiness out of which it arises.

It is not really possible to have only experiences that we would personally put into the category of spiritual experiences. But every experience, no matter how mundane it may seem, can become an experience of enlightenment or *awareness* when we finally drop all these definitions of spiritual or unspiritual and come to see that what we experience is not really the point at all. In the path of *awareness*, we are not primarily concerned with *what* we experience, but with the simple fact *that* we experience. All we need to do to live a truly awakened life is to recognize this fact more and more in the midst of any and every experience.

Even the most sublime experience of enlightenment, like all experiences, will come and go. It does
not matter so much whether or not we can point to
a specific date and time and say: *On December 3rd,
1956, at four in the afternoon, at the corner of Chelsea
and 5th St in New York City, I was Fully Enlightened.*
So what? Your enlightenment is only as good as your
present- moment, direct experience of liberating *awareness.* If your experience becomes a big story with which
you begin to identify and then you build a sense of self
around it, then guess what? You are going to suffer.
And remember that the Buddha's working definition of
enlightenment was that it was the end of suffering.

Can't you see how the most perfect *awareness*
can't help but be effortlessly and eternally present? It
is as effortlessly present as your very existence itself.
In fact, *awareness* and existence are not two different
things at all. *Awareness* is your most basic sense of
existence-consciousness. *Awareness* or existence is the
fundamental *I am* that must always be eternally present for anything at all to be present. It is the formless-
ness out of which and on which, every form is built.
Just as a building cannot exist without a foundation,
so no form can exist without the foundation of formless *awareness.*

So to return to the question that makes up this
chapter title: on a very practical level, *What would be
the simplest approach to noticing this awareness that is
always present?* The most simple practice instruction
that I can come up with can actually be contained in
one word, spoken in the imperative. This is probably
the most simple spiritual practice instruction you will
ever receive, and as long as it is not misinterpreted, it is
sufficient in itself. The word is:

Relax.

'Call off the search' is a phrase that often comes up in discussions about non-duality. And, if properly understood, it can work as a spiritual teaching. But people often think that calling off the search means that, as there is nothing to do and everyone is already perfectly aware and enlightened, we can just carry on living in our same stuck and unsatisfactory patterns, whilst considering ourselves fully awakened. But this is a misunderstanding of both the instruction to call off the search and the instruction to *relax*. So maybe, as a clarification of the instruction to relax, I will add just two more little words to the one word *relax*. So now the more 'advanced' instruction would be the following:

Relax and notice.

If you simply relax and notice the *awareness* that is always in the background of any experience you could possibly ever have, every experience, any form that arises, without exception, can point to the pure *awareness* you seek. Every single experience you have, any thought, perception or situation, will always, inexorably, unfailingly, inevitably lead you back to the beautiful, pure *awareness* that you have actually never lacked.

Shift Attention, Relax and Notice.

OK, now the spiritual practice instruction has gone up to five words. It's still pretty simple, wouldn't you say?

✳ CHAPTER 8

THINK ABOUT WHAT YOU THINK ABOUT

As a person thinks in their heart, so are they.

Hebrew proverb

We have been talking a lot about happiness: how it is innate and is, in reality, our own essential, true nature as God's children. We have said that happiness is not caused by obtaining the many things we desire. If any of the millions of fleeting pleasures you have experienced in your lifetime could bring true and stable happiness, don't you think you would be happy by now? We have said that happiness is found within, not without, and it is important as well to understand that unhappiness is also not the result of things coming or going outside ourselves. Unhappiness is not caused by people, places, things, situations or circumstances. Unhappiness is actually caused by negative thoughts about people, places, things, situations or circumstances. Negative thoughts are the real cause of unhappiness. Reality is not the problem—thinking is. It is the stories you tell yourself about reality that make it appear to be a problem sometimes. All problems are actually mind-created.

If happiness is innate, it is essential to who you really are at the deepest level, it is always with you, always present. Remember, that is the meaning of the word 'essential'. Whatever is essential to a thing must always exist for the thing itself to exist. So happiness is never absent from us. Somewhere along the way, we just stopped noticing it. So, if I am perpetually, eternally happy, why is it that I don't always feel so happy?

Consider the sun. The sun is always shining in the heavens. It always shines with the same intensity. It never stops shining or decides to go hide in the core of the earth instead of staying up in the heavens. Yet we don't always experience the sun, do we? Why is that? It's pretty simple really. The earth is always rotating on its axis. When one side of the earth rotates toward the sun, it is considered daytime on that side of the earth. When the earth rotates away from the sun, it has its back to the sun, so to speak. On the side of the earth that is not facing the sun, it is considered night time. At that time, doesn't it seem that no effects of the sun exist at all? Yet we know that a certain warmth from the sun is still present, even on the night side of the earth. Otherwise, at night, the side of the earth not facing the sun would die. It would become a frozen, absolutely cold hell realm. Even at night, light from the sun still exists, reflected by the moon. The sun also seems not to exist when the sky becomes cloudy and covers it over. On a cloudy day is the sun deciding not to shine? Has it taken a day off and abandoned the earth? No. For behind even the darkest sky, the sun continues to shine with the full force of its radiance. It always remains beautiful, warm and radiant—it is simply temporarily covered over by clouds.

Our interpretations of reality, the stories we continually tell ourselves about people, places, things or circumstances, are like the clouds in the sky of our consciousness. They cover over the shining *presence of God* within us that is our own essential, true nature as God's children. Just like the sun in the sky, our true nature is always shining. Its very nature is to radiate pure happiness. So, happiness is never really absent from us—it is just covered over sometimes.

Another way we cover over our innate joyfulness is when we turn our back on it, just as the earth turns its back on the sun each night. We turn our back on the essential joy of our true nature when we look in the wrong direction for happiness. We believe—because everyone has told us so—that happiness is not already within us, but instead needs to be acquired through obtaining more things from outside ourselves. Remember Jesus' parable of the prodigal son? It teaches us that when we are not looking in the right place for something we have lost, we will never find it. It teaches that, when we turn our back on our own true nature by looking for happiness in things, people, places or circumstances, it will seem sometimes that happiness itself does not exist for us. And, in a certain sense, it doesn't exist for us at that moment. At least we are not experiencing it in that moment. So, even though it never ceased to shine at the very core of our being, we were not aware of it. So, for us, it didn't exist.

Here is an example of this: Let's say you bought a winning lottery ticket and placed it in your bottom desk drawer and forgot all about it. The lottery numbers came in that very night and you won seventy million dollars. However, you rarely watch TV or listen to the radio and you forgot to check the winning lottery numbers in the paper that night. So you remain completely unaware that you are a multimillionaire. During the following months you come on some hard times. You lose your job. You have to leave your apartment because you can't pay the rent. Even your car breaks down. Then the repo-man comes to get it anyway because you were unable to keep up the car payments. What a life! Yet the whole time you were a millionaire. You were simply unaware of this fact—so you were living like a poor person and suffering from the consequences of being a poor person. The story you were telling yourself was that you were poor. But in reality you weren't poor at all. You were rich beyond your wildest dreams. Yet you had no experience of your wealth because you didn't know about it. For you the seventy million didn't exist.

We all tell ourselves stories about reality every day. Some of the stories are old ones we learned as children. Some are new stories we just learned yesterday or five minutes ago. Some are nice stories, some are not so nice. One spiritual practice we can take up is to learn to question our stories about life. When we begin to question our stories and ask ourselves if this is really true, we begin to see that it is truly not our experiences in life that are making us unhappy—it is simply the story we're telling ourselves about the experience that is the culprit.

I once had an experience as a hospital chaplain that illustrates this truth very well. The floor I was working on at the time was a cardiac surgery floor. The patients on this particular floor had mostly had open heart surgery involving a coronary artery bypass to clear the blood flow to the heart. There were two women patients I visited whose rooms were side by side. They were about the same age (early forties), from a similar educational background (both had graduated from the same local college), both had two children, a nice house in the suburbs, and both had just undergone triple bypass surgery. One of the women, whom we will call Alice, decided that it was a blessing she had had a severe chest pain, went to the hospital emergency room and discovered she was in need of the bypass surgery. She kept saying, "This situation saved my life. The doctor told me I could have had a major heart attack at any time and would quite probably have simply dropped dead without this surgery. I am so grateful all this happened." Alice was a pleasure to be around. She felt she had been given another chance at life. She was grateful for everything. She praised the kindness of the hospital staff, loved her doctors and constantly told them how much she appreciated them. She even loved the hospital food.

The lady in the room next to her, whose surface life and basic personal profile seemed so similar to Alice's, we will call Carol. Carol complained bitterly about how the staff were treating her, felt that being forced to stay in the hospital was like being stuck in a prison, was angry at God that she had to suffer such a serious medical set-back at the age of forty-two and hated, with extreme loathing, the hospital food.

Which of these women had the correct view of reality? Actually neither had the correct view of reality—they simply had their own view of reality. They both told themselves a story about what had happened to their heart. One story was a nice, hopeful story. One story was not so nice.

And what stories about life are you currently telling yourself? Are they nice stories, sad stories, happy stories or depressing stories? You can learn by investigating all your stories that actually none of them are real in any absolute sense. Of course it's more pleasant to tell yourself happy stories rather than sad ones. Once on a retreat I participated in, an old Jesuit priest said something funny in this regard. He said that pessimists are out of touch with reality. Optimists are equally out of touch with reality—but optimists have more fun.

Sooner or later, though, optimist or pessimist, you can come to the point where you realize directly that all the stories we tell ourselves are ultimately never completely true. You will come to realize that the perfect happiness you seek is not to be found, even in the happiest story. Perfect happiness actually has no cause. That's right. Perfect happiness is never the effect of an efficient cause. Perfect, unconditional happiness is the joy of *being* itself. Perfect happiness is who you really are at the core of your being.

There are three aspects of life I would like to share with you that illustrate how thinking (one of these three aspects) works in creating your basic experience of life. Understanding these three simple aspects can teach you how to uncover all the happiness and peace you are looking for. All you have to do is understand clearly how these aspects work together interdependently and together form your fundamental perception of life, which in turn creates whatever experience of life you may have. These three aspects are general life-principles that are universal and generic. In other words, they work in just the same way for everyone all the time, no matter what religion, nationality, culture or background they may come from. Understanding these three, simple aspects of life and applying this understanding to your daily life can greatly help you in the discovery of the innate happiness and peace that is already always yours as God's beloved child.

The three aspects of life are:

1. The Aspect of *Awareness*
2. The Aspect of *Thinking*
3. The Aspect of *Feelings/Emotions*

Awareness

The aspect of *awareness* reflects the understanding that, in the deepest core of your being itself, you are already aware and the essential nature of this *awareness* is happiness, peace and joy. You will never actually find happiness by seeking it in people, places or things because, the moment you start seeking it there, you imply that it is to be found outside instead of within you. You will discover this innate happiness when you learn to let go of the attachment to and identification with the thinking and emotions that are obscuring it. This simple, present-moment *awareness* that you are is not separate from the *presence of God* within you and everyone else, as the very ground or backdrop of *being*. That's why I sometimes call it your true nature as God's beloved child.

Thinking

The aspect of *thinking* reflects the understanding that thinking is simply a function of human consciousness that can be used to assist you in carrying out certain practical objectives that are just a normal part of life—activities such as doing a math problem, planning a schedule or a trip, balancing your checkbook. Thinking is in its right place when it is be used as a tool in carrying out these practical actions and then put away when you are done using it. But most of us, for a big segment of our lives, never learn how to put away this tool of thought. Instead we identify with all these thoughts and think that is who we are, instead of the pure, present-moment, simple *awareness* that we really are. These non-functional thoughts with which we identify and that obscure our true nature of pure *awareness* are judgmental thoughts, bitter complaining, whining, self-pitying thoughts, thoughts of making demands that some person, place or thing should be or not be a certain way, defeatist, pessimistic thinking. In other words, all the egoic, negative thoughts which habitually run through many people's consciousness on a pretty regular basis. These kinds of dysfunctional thoughts obscure the peace and joy of our true nature by taking our focus off the present-moment, pure *awareness* where our true nature is always abiding.

Feelings/Emotions

The aspect of *feelings/emotions* reflects the understanding that our feelings/emotions act as indicators of whether or not we are believing any of the dysfunctional thinking that may be arising in *awareness*. If we believe such dysfunctional thoughts we will feel bad because, by so doing, we are allowing such thoughts effectively to cover over or obscure the radiant joy and peace of our true nature as pure *awareness*. If we understand that such thoughts are not who we really are, and are simply thoughts, we allow them to arise and cease in the space of pure, silent *awareness*, and they are no big deal at all. Any thought whatsoever can come and go in the space of pure *awareness* and the *awareness* itself is wholly unaffected by it. This simple allowing of thoughts to come and go in the spacious *awareness* that you are is learning how to put away the tool of thought, when it has served its necessary purpose. This frees you from the identification with thoughts and introduces you to the liberation of pure, spacious *awareness* in the present moment, which is who you really are.

Let's look at a possible, everyday experience of thinking that may help illustrate this matter of the three aspects. Suppose you were having a wonderful Christmas dinner with many close friends and relatives. Some of these people live nearby and are a regular part of your daily life. Others are living far away and have traveled quite a long distance to be at this special event. The one thing all these people have in common for you, is that they are all people whom you dearly love. Everyone is having a wonderful time; the conversation is lively and joyous. Let's say at this point it begins to rain and storm outside. It's raining cats and dogs. Are you going to allow a bunch of negative, complaining thoughts about the rain to enter your consciousness and begin whining to all your relatives and friends who will listen about how bad the rain is? Of course you won't. You are not about to allow a little rain to spoil such a wonderful, special, enjoyable event, are you? You simply let such thoughts go and return to the wonderful party.

Or let's say you are at a noisy restaurant having a wonderful and important conversation with someone you love. Are you going to stop giving your loved one any attention and focus instead on all the noise going on around you? Of course not. You simply tune out all the noise and distraction and you gaze into the eyes of the one you love and focus completely on their presence before you.

So likewise, once we clearly see that the simple presence of present-moment *awareness* is our natural, innate source of happiness and peace in life, that it is the very *presence of God* within us, we will allow nothing at all, especially just a little thought, to distract us from it.

And what tips us off that we may be allowing some of these dysfunctional thoughts to distract us from the pure *awareness* of our true nature? It is our feelings or emotions that tip us off. When we are feeling trapped in a low mood or just generally bad or negative, we can be sure that we are engaged with believing in some thought, or series of thoughts, that is obscuring our pure *awareness*. We have bought into the idea that some stuff that is merely passing through our head is who we are, and have momentarily forgotten that who we really are, is this innate pure, simple *awareness* in the present moment. We have allowed our thoughts to veil the paradise that dwells within us as the *presence of God*.

The tragic thing about this is how totally unnecessary it all is. The presence of spacious, present-moment *awareness* is the source of all the happiness we are seeking somewhere out there. We need look no further than our most basic, natural sense of existence, or beingness, here and now. And yet, we have somehow learned to ignore the joy and peace within and focus instead on that which takes us away from it. How crazy is this?

This spacious, natural sense of happy beingness in the present moment is our true nature as God's beloved child. It is the good news that is at the core of the teaching of Jesus and all awakened children of God. To call God, our Father-Mother is to say that God is the source of our very being itself. This simple *awareness*, that is always content simply being in the eternal *now* of God, is God's presence. It is the *presence of God* at the very center of our being and it has never left us. Why turn away from it? Why ignore it? It's like ignoring our loved one in the noisy restaurant. Why would we do such a thing? Simply shift your attention a bit and notice it. Notice that precious *awareness* that is always, eternally present here and now.

Do you, by chance, remember that simple, little song by Bobby McFerrin that came out in the mid-eighties? It was so simple that a lot of people made fun of it. They wondered how a song almost entirely consisting of one, simple refrain could become so popular. The title of the song (and the majority of the lyrics) was one, simple line: "Don't worry, be happy."

Pretty uncomplicated, isn't it? But there is a profound and liberating teaching contained in these simple words.

So here, again, are the three aspects of life:

Awareness: Your true nature of present-moment *awareness* is happiness itself. Don't take my word for this. Just begin to notice it and find out for yourself.

Thoughts: Believing instead that you are your thoughts and identifying with them brings an experience of unhappiness, worry and anxiety into your life. You are not your thoughts. Thoughts are just thoughts.

Feelings/emotions: Your negative, bad feelings/emotions are your tip-off that you are identifying with some thought or other that you simply need to let go of. You simply are not this thought. Relax, let go of the thought, notice and rest in the ever present *awareness* that is your true nature as God's beloved child.

Rest in that which is aware of all the thoughts that come and go. This *awareness* is who you really are.

CHAPTER 9

THE WAY OF THE CROSS

The cross is the universal symbol of the Christian faith. No matter where you go in the world, wherever there are Christians of whatever type or denomination, there is the cross: crosses on church roofs, crosses outside churches, crosses inside churches and chapels, crosses around Christians' necks. Catholic, Orthodox and Anglican Christians (and I have even seen some evangelical Christians) make the sign of the cross by touching their forehead, chest and each shoulder as they say, "In the name of the Father, Son and the Holy Spirit," at the beginning and end of religious services.

So clearly the cross is, perhaps arguably, the central symbol of Christianity. Yet, originally, the cross was simply an instrument of torture, humiliation and execution. In ancient Roman and Jewish culture it would be seen as anything but a holy or sacred symbol. The cross was associated with criminals, crime and punishment and painful death, much like the electric chair would be seen today as such a negative symbol of suffering and death. But there is a deep universal truth that is contained in the symbol of the cross that perhaps we rarely think about. As we have said, the cross was actually an instrument that was used for human execution. It has become so sacrosanct that we often forget this fact. But anyone who saw the movie *The Passion of the Christ* has some idea of what the cross originally symbolized for most people in the ancient societies in which it was used to execute criminals.

But the meaning and symbolism behind the cross can be seen differently today.

There probably aren't many human experiences that are comparable to crucifixion. It would most certainly have been an extreme experience of intense powerlessness, pain, humiliation and agonizing physical and psychological suffering. On one level, as an instrument of torture and humiliation, the cross symbolizes the most extreme human weakness and sense of vulnerability, but as a symbol of spiritual transcendence the cross of Jesus teaches us the transforming power of self-surrender and the victory of love over hatred.

There is nothing more natural and normal than to recoil from the experience of physical pain. The resistance to suffering is universal in human beings and even in other life forms like animals and insects. It is perfectly natural and healthy to avoid situations of pain when they can be avoided. Yet when you can do nothing to prevent or alleviate the pain you are experiencing in the moment, you can learn to let go of even this quite natural form of resistance and allow instead the experience of suffering to simply be there. As you do this, you will notice the spaciousness of *awareness* in which the pain is arising and not just the pain itself. When you learn to surrender, even in the midst of deep human suffering, as Jesus did on the cross, you learn to experience whatever arises willingly, as if you yourself had actually chosen it. Jesus expressed this spirit of surrender when he prayed, "Not my will but Thy will be done." And, "Into your hands I commend my spirit."

This is the transforming miracle to which the symbol of the cross of Jesus points—that within every experience that, on the surface, seems to be clearly evil, bad or at the very least undesirable, there is a hidden deeper good. That deeper good can reveal itself both interiorly or exteriorly when there is true self-surrender and acceptance of whatever *is*. When, through self-surrender, you are in a nonreactive relationship to whatever arrives in the present moment, you transcend the labels of good and bad and you come to the realization that "everything works together for good to those who love God".

There is a theory in physics called the butterfly effect: If a butterfly on a distant shore flaps its wings the course of history may be changed. This idea about how reality functions as an interconnected whole reflects the oneness of all of life. It sees that nothing happens in a vacuum. There are no isolated events; it only appears to be so. This way of understanding reality sees it as a universal wholeness where everything is part of the great matrix of interconnectedness that we call the cosmos. And though we don't always see it or appreciate it, all is unfolding according to a greater plan for the greater good. This means that whatever is could not have been different. When we practice self-surrender we trust this unfolding of the universe, even when it seems to touch us personally in ways we don't particularly like or may find painful or unpleasant.

The self-surrender of Jesus on the cross teaches us by graphic example that true surrender is surrender to whatever arrives in this moment. Your surrender is not to the story you are telling yourself as an interpretation of this moment. For example, you may have a serious disability, like blindness or paralysis. This condition is what it is. Maybe your story to yourself about this condition is a sad upsetting one that says: *Why do such terrible things always happen to me?* But if you can learn to accept just *what is* and drop the sad story about it, you will once again notice your *awareness* of the pain and not merely the pain itself. You know that self-surrender has finally arrived when you no longer find the question *why me?* to be a compelling question. The real question is *why* not *me?*

And once again, this is not to say you should simply passively accept all situations in the sense of doing nothing about them. Not at all. Certain situations are calling you precisely to respond and do something to initiate change of some kind. If illness or disability come your way then you will do what you need to do for healing or improved function. But, on a purely interior level, when you practice self-surrender, there is an acceptance that, yes, at the moment this is the way this situation is. I hope I can change it, I have faith that it will indeed change for the better, but right now, this is the way it is. Sometimes it takes a severe situation to teach you that true peace, the peace that passes all understanding, is not based at all on any condition being any certain way whatsoever. You learn that the truest peace and happiness is completely unconditional just as true love is unconditional.

In his beautiful little book *Stillness Speaks*, Eckhart Tolle writes:

Throughout history there have been women and men who, in the face of great loss, illness, imprisonment, or impending death, accepted the seemingly unacceptable and thus found the 'peace that passes

*all understanding'. Acceptance of the unacceptable
is the greatest source of grace in this world.*

The other great lesson that is contained in the crucifixion of Jesus is the teaching about how love always
triumphs over hatred. It is not, as some might think,
an object lesson on good triumphing over evil. Jesus
did not see those who crucified him as evil. He didn't
say from the cross: *I curse you all, you miserable, evil
people, you rotten sinners. I hate you all for killing me
unjustly.* No, these were not the words found on the
lips of Jesus in the Gospel accounts. Instead he said,
"Father, forgive them, they have no idea what it is they
are doing." He didn't even see his own murderers as
malicious, but simply as misguided and ignorant. This
offers us a graphic example of Jesus' understanding
of the practice of forgiveness and unconditional love.
Such love can transform and heal the world. Look at
the power of love manifested in the lives of a Gandhi or
a Martin Luther King, in Mother Teresa, Saint Francis
or the Dalai Lama. In all of these lives it is the same
Christ-love radiating out into the world.

These are the great lessons of self-surrender and
the power of unconditional love that the cross of Jesus
points to. When we see the power of grace working in
such an extreme situation as the crucifixion of Jesus
we can more easily see it in the less extreme situations
of vulnerability or hatred we are likely to encounter in
our own everyday lives. The next time we see a cross
on a church, on a sign somewhere, or around someone's
neck, we can think of the teachings of love and self-
surrender that Jesus taught, not only in words, but
through the witness of his very life and death. This is
a grace that is truly redemptive. Being redemptive, it

saves us from the seeming power of hatred and teaches us that in the end light will always swallow up the darkness and love always overcomes hatred.

This great lesson was the true sacrifice of Jesus on the cross. His death on the cross saves us because it teaches us how to allow *what is*, to accept *what is* and eventually to actually love *what is*. This is more than a superficial, passive milk-and-water acceptance of fate—it is a profoundly dynamic allowing, a deep acceptance. Ultimately, in loving *what is*, we are loving God himself, we are loving our own true Self.

✳ CHAPTER 10

THE PUREST TEACHING IS SILENCE

In the silence of the heart, God speaks.

Blessed Mother Teresa of Calcutta

The purest teaching is silence. This will be the briefest of chapters in this book because it arose quite simply out of one of the morning times of silent stillness and peace. It would seem incongruous to make many words and concepts about this inarticulate, silent regard that lifts one above thought. I hope the stillness that permeates these few words will point you in the direction of silence and encourage you to rest there in the silent gaze of love yourself. This is the wordless gaze that rests with eyes wide open and aware, yet is not looking on anything except that which is itself looking. Just be quiet and rest in silent stillness. No more is really needed than this. For some, these words may seem obscure or abstract, but they are pointing more directly to the silence and urging you to return to it more clearly than all the other words that are here written.

Be aware of the silent watcher that sees through the eyes but cannot be seen.

Be aware of that which hears through the ears,

but cannot be heard, that which knows but cannot be known as an object. One knows it only by *being* it. Just *be* the silent *awareness* that sees, hears, tastes, smells, touches. Just become conscious of that which is conscious. Be conscious of consciousness itself. Become aware of *awareness* before it is aware of anything in particular. This silent watcher and listener is always still, without words, without thought. It is the silent, alert *awareness* that is there before any thought arises and is there after all thought subsides.

This silent stillness is who you are and it is never separate from God. This silence is always present, even in the midst of chaos and noise. This is the *now I am*. Return again and again to this silence.

I say, return, but in reality you have never left the silence, you just stopped noticing it, even though you *are* it. When you return to silence you are actually returning to your deepest Self. You are the prodigal returning to the house of the father. Your real journey in life is always interior. When the mind is turned within to the *now I am*, the noise of the world begins to fade in the bright light of *awareness*.

The happiness you seek can never be found in anything this world can offer.

This is not to say you must renounce the world or not enjoy the good things life has to offer. You just come to realize that none of them can ever bring the absolute happiness and bliss you were created to contain within you. In actual fact you can stop seeking at any time since what you seek is what is seeking. What you are looking for is the one who is looking right now at these words on this page. That's the reason it seems so difficult to find, it's here already, as close as hands and feet.

Your true Self is *awareness* before it is aware of any object. The true Self is silence, stillness, peace. Simply rest in that as much as you can. Look beyond thinking and sensing. Thinking and sensing are temporary and so are not real at all on an absolute level. But the simple awareness of the *now I am* is eternal, unchanging and filled with unconditional happiness and unbounded joy. Rest in the serene silence of this Self. Abide there always. That is who you have always been and who you will always be in this one eternal *now* of God.

If you have ever tasted this silence, return to it again and again. Eventually you will realize that there has never been anywhere else to go, and there you will remain. To live always conscious of this consciousness, to live forever aware of this *awareness*, is itself the great *awareness*. This inner stillness and peace is the Christ within, the mind that was in Christ Jesus. Let this mind be in you, the mind that is no-mind. This profound silence and stillness is itself the true Self, the supreme identity which is no-identity, the consciousness of the indwelling Christ, the true Self which is no-self. Just be that always. Be who you are. After all, who else could you possibly ever be? Be silent and then listen to that silence without any words at all. If you don't understand that silence you won't understand the true import of a single word in this book, not really. Because the purest teaching is silence.

Recent and Forthcoming Books
from
Non-Duality Press

THE SUN RISES IN THE EVENING *by* Gary Nixon PhD
Beyond addiction and limited recovery

EMPTINESS AND JOYFUL FREEDOM
Greg Gooode & Tomas Sander

FULL STOP! THE GATEWAY TO PRESENT PERFECTION
by John Wheeler

THE HEAVENLY BACKFLIP
by JC Amberchele

THE WORLD IS MY MIRROR
by Richard Bates

GONER *by* Louis Brawley
The Final Travels of UG Krishnamurti

NOTHING TO GRASP *by* Joan Tollifson

SILENCE HEALS *by* Yolande Duran-Serrano

THE DIRECT PATH *by* Greg Goode

A FLOWER IN THE DESERT
by Richard lang

CONSCIOUS.TV is a TV channel which broadcasts on the Internet at www.conscious.tv. It also has programmes shown on several satellite and cable channels round the world including the Sky system in the UK where you can watch programmes at 9pm every evening on channel No 275. The channel aims to stimulate debate, question, enquire, inform, enlighten, encourage and inspire people in the areas of Consciousness, Non-Duality and Science. It also has a section called 'Life Stories' with many fascinating interviews.

There are over 200 interviews to watch including several with communicators on Non-Duality including Jeff Foster, Steve Ford, Suzanne Foxton, Gangaji, Greg Goode, Scott Kiloby, Richard Lang, Francis Lucille, Roger Linden, Wayne Liquorman, Jac O'Keefe, Mooji, Catherine Noyce, Tony Parsons, Halina Pytlasinska, Genpo Roshi, Satyananda, Richard Sylvester, Rupert Spira, Florian Schlosser, Mandi Solk, James Swartz, and Pamela Wilson. There is also an interview with UG Krishnamurti. Some of these interviewees also have books available from Non-Duality Press.

Do check out the channel as we are interested in your feedback and any ideas you may have for future programmes. Email us at info@conscious.tv with your ideas or if you would like to be on our email newsletter list.

WWW.CONSCIOUS.TV

CONSCIOUS.TV and NON-DUALITY PRESS
present two unique DVD releases

CONVERSATIONS ON NON-DUALITY – VOLUME 1
Tony Parsons – The Open Secret • Rupert Spira –
The Transparency of Things – Parts 1 & 2 • Richard Lang –
Seeing Who You Really Are

CONVERSATIONS ON NON-DUALITY – VOLUME 2
Jeff Foster – Life Without a Centre • Richard Sylvester –
I Hope You Die Soon • Roger Linden – The Elusive Obvious

Available to order from: www.non-dualitypress.org

CONVERSATIONS ON NON-DUALITY
Twenty-Six Awakenings

The book explores the nature of true happiness, awakening, enlightenment and the 'Self' to be realised. It features 26 expressions of liberation, each shaped by different life experiences and offering a unique perspective.

The collection explores the different ways 'liberation' happened and 'suffering' ended. Some started with therapy, self-help workshops or read books written by spiritual masters, while others travelled to exotic places and studied with gurus. Others leapt from the despair of addiction to drugs and alcohol to simply waking up unexpectedly to a new reality.

The 26 interviews included in the book are with: David Bingham, Daniel Brown, Sundance Burke, Katie Davis, Peter Fenner, Steve Ford, Jeff Foster, Suzanne Foxton, Gagaji, Richard Lang, Roger Linden, Wayne Liquorman, Francis Lucille, Mooji, Catherine Noyce, Jac O'Keeffe, Tony Parsons, Bernie Prior, Halina Pytlasinska, Genpo Roshi, Florian Schlosser, Mandi Solk, Rupert Spira, James Swartz, Richard Sylvester and Pamela Wilson.

CPSIA information can be obtained at www.ICGtesting.com
Printed in the USA
LVOW11s1752031214

416961LV00007B/1037/P